RADICAL
THINKING

RADICAL THINKING

How to see the bigger picture

PETER LAMONT

Swift

SWIFT PRESS

First published in Great Britain by Swift Press 2024

1 3 5 7 9 8 6 4 2

Copyright © Peter Lamont 2024

The right of Peter Lamont to be identified as the Author of this Work has been asserted in accordance with the Copyright, Designs and Patents Act 1988.

Typeset by Tetragon, London
Printed and bound in Great Britain by CPI Group (UK) Ltd, Croydon CR0 4YY

A CIP catalogue record for this book is available from the British Library

ISBN: 9781800751347
eISBN: 9781800751354

For my parents, who will never read it.[1]

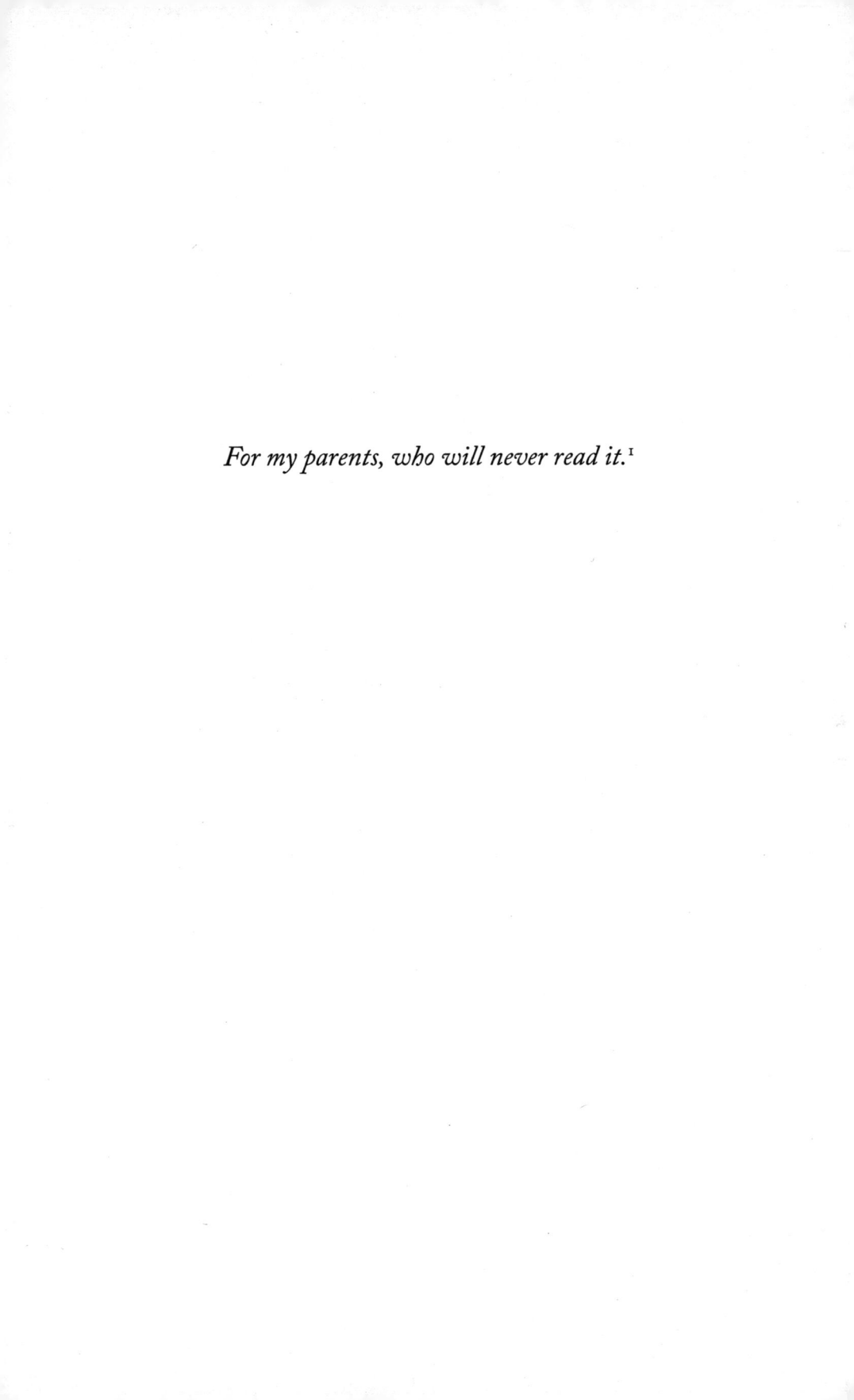

CONTENTS

The Curiosity Shop   9

PART 1: THE WINDOW THROUGH WHICH YOU LOOK

Where to start?   15

1. What we notice   21
2. A limited picture   37
3. How we interpret things   53
4. Our points of view   77
5. Local customs and habits   96
6. Tools of persuasion   118
7. How we feel   137
8. What we want   153

PART 2: THINKING IN A RADICAL WAY

9. Where are we?   175
10. The limits of logic   184
11. The boundaries of science   202
12. You can make sense of anything   222

Exit: Beyond the square   241

Acknowledgements   247

Notes   249

THE CURIOSITY SHOP

In the Old Town of Edinburgh, many years ago, there was a shop that sold curiosities.

Every day, as people walked by the shop, they looked in the window. They looked at the curious things on display. The alluring oddities, enticing knick-knacks and bizarre novelties captured their attention. However, nobody went into the shop.

Day after day, people looked in the window. They looked, from the same position, at whatever curious things were on display. They preferred some things to others. But nobody went into the shop.

Then, one day, a curious child passed by. She looked at the things on display. She saw them all through the same window. Naturally, she preferred some things to others. However, she was curious. So, after a while, she noticed something else. It was something that nobody else had noticed…

She noticed the window through which she was looking.

That was when she realised that it was displaying a limited number of things. It was presenting them in a particular way. And, being a curious child, she wondered what she was missing. She wanted to see things from different angles.

So, she decided to go into the shop.

Radical Thinking

This is a book about being more curious. It's about noticing the window through which you look – the window that frames your view of the world.

As you try to make sense of the world around you, you begin with what's on display. You notice a limited number of things. You see them from a particular position. Naturally, you prefer some things to others. In the process, you form a world-view.

It is, of course, a restricted view. Whatever you think – about *any* subject at all – it's based on what you notice and how you interpret what you see and hear. It's based on limited information, which is presented to you in a particular way, and on your personal preferences. Whatever your view of the world might be, this is the window through which you look. It limits your view and frames what you see. In other words, it shapes your thoughts.

Beyond this, there's a bigger picture. To see it, you need to be more curious. You need to wonder about what you're missing. You need to look at things from different angles. You need to realise the limits of your view.

The limits of your view are far from obvious. After all, we now have access to more information than at any time in history. However, we live in a world of urgent noise. Alluring offers, enticing pitches and bizarre claims capture our attention. We're intrigued by the latest meme and drawn to competing truths from rival factions. The problem isn't a lack of information. The problem is how to make sense of it all.

This requires some radical thinking.

We're not in control of the endless noise that fills our eyes and ears. Nevertheless, whatever we see and hear, it's up to us to make sense of it. To do that, we need to remember our limits. There are things that shape our thoughts, which aren't out there in the world that we see. They're in the ways that we see the world. And *that* is something that's in our control. But, to realise our limits, we need to be more curious about how, in general, we see things.

We look at the world, of course, from wherever we are. I'm here. You're somewhere else. Your view of the world is different from mine. Nevertheless, the things that shape your world-view are the same things that shape mine.

This is a book about these things. It's about what you see, and what you miss, and how you can look farther and see things differently. It's about what you believe, what you take for granted, what you find convincing, how you feel, and what you want. It's a local guide to how you think about everything. In the end, it's about how you can make sense of anything.

And it starts here.

The only question is: Are you curious?

PART I

The Window Through Which You Look

WHERE TO START?

The Radical Road is out of bounds. We're told that the route is too dangerous.

The Radical Road is a rocky path. It takes you up the side of a hill near the centre of Edinburgh. It was built after the Radical War of 1820. The Radicals were fighting for the right to vote. At the time, only one in five hundred Scots could vote. The Radicals lost. The leaders were arrested, denounced as traitors, and then they were hanged and beheaded. The remaining radical rascals were recruited to create this recreational road.[1] Since then, it's been called the Radical Road.

If you walked up the Radical Road today, you would get a better view. You would be able to see farther. You would see the surrounding area from different angles. So, as you looked around, you would see your position within the bigger picture. The Radical Road provides perspective.

But not today. The path is closed. The authorities are concerned about falling rocks. At the moment, it's considered too dangerous.[2]

The Radical Road may be closed, but the path to more radical thinking is not.

Radical Thinking

Radical thinking is a matter of perspective. It depends on what you take for granted. For example, the Radicals thought that *all* men – but *only* men – should be able to vote. Two centuries ago, this was radical stuff. It was considered dangerous. But not today. From today's perspective, they weren't radical enough.

Whatever your current view of the world – about politics, religion or anything else – you can think in a more radical way. You can look farther. You can look at things from different angles. This provides a sense of perspective. And today, in this world of competing distractions and rival truths, this is needed more than ever.

The Radicals had political aims. But the radical thinking to which I refer isn't particularly political. It's 'radical' (from *radic*, meaning *root*) because it's about questioning the basics: the things that you take for granted. It's about noticing the window through which you look at the world, and how this shapes your thoughts.

If you're not curious about this, then you'll continue to have a limited view. You'll not see beyond your current position. You'll be missing the bigger picture.

It's becoming increasingly difficult to see beyond our current positions. We're constantly telling others what we think. We post and tweet and share our views. We wear them on badges, caps and T-shirts. We express them in public and identify with them. As we do, we take sides – we think *this* not *that* – and then we defend our territory. We justify what we think and, as we reject the views of others, we fail to understand why *they* would think *that*. We accuse each other of ignorance, or bias, or bad intentions, for thinking differently. We become trapped in an endless series of arguments that reinforce our own opinions.

And yet, for over a century, psychologists have been pointing out how we get things wrong. According to psychologists, you're flawed in your thinking. Your perception is faulty. You make bad decisions. You're an irrational creature who's riddled with biases. Your thoughts are dictated by your brain, that remarkable but mischievous lump of flesh over which you have little, if any, control. So, whatever you happen to think, how can you possibly know that you're right?

The best solution, according to many, is to engage in 'critical thinking'. This is often presented as some rules that you can follow, which will help you to get it right. For most critical thinking experts, these are the rules of logic and the methods of science. You're encouraged to learn about the logical fallacies and the countless biases to which you're prone – because they lead to erroneous conclusions.[3]

Now, the rules of logic and the methods of science are fine things to learn. However, as we'll see, they have their limits. And you can certainly learn about the logical fallacies and the countless biases to which you're prone. But you still won't know if what you think is right. In the abstract world of logic, of course, where the rules are fixed, you can spot an error. In the controlled world of the scientific experiment, where the facts are known, you can spot a bias. However, you don't live in either of those worlds.

You live in the real and uncertain world of limited information, questionable data, rival views and competing interests. Whatever you see or hear, at any given time, it's not obvious which rules are in play or, for that matter, which facts are true. In the real world, whatever you think, you can never be sure if your conclusion is right. So, what on earth are you to think?

Radical Thinking

You need to think in a more radical way: it's not about *what* you think.

Thinking is a process, not an outcome. It's a path that you take until you reach a conclusion. Along the way, you're guided by limited information, which is presented from a particular angle, and by your personal preferences ... until, at some point, you stop. You arrive at a position. This is what you think. This is the outcome.

To think in a critical way, however, you need to think about the process. When critical thinking is pitched as a way to reach the right outcome, this itself is an error. Critical thinking isn't about *what* you think: it's about *how* you think.[4] Whatever the outcome, it's about how you got there. And, to make sense of the views of others, you need to understand how they got to where they are.

As we walked the path to our current positions, we were all guided by limited information, particular angles and personal preferences. It's never just a matter of facts. Nobody knows all the facts and, whatever the facts, they must be interpreted. It's not just a matter of bias. None of us is neutral. No wonder that we disagree.

But we needn't agree on what we think.

If you wish to make sense of what's going on, then you need to get past *what* you think. You need to understand *how* you arrived at that thought. You need to question what you take for granted. You need to notice the less obvious things that guide your thoughts and frame your view. You need to see your position within the bigger picture. This provides a sense of perspective from which you can make sense of everything else.

So, where to start?

We look at the world from wherever we are. I'm here. You're somewhere else. But this isn't about your current view, whatever it might be. It's about *how* we look at things. Frankly, we could start from anywhere. But I'm here, so let's start from where I am.

At the moment, I'm in George Square, which is near the centre of Edinburgh. From here, I can see the Radical Road. It's less than a mile away. However, as I mentioned earlier, that path is currently out of bounds. So, I can start from here. It doesn't really matter. As you'll soon see, it's not really about here.

In part one, I'm going to walk around George Square, and tell you about some local curiosities. I'm going to use these to reveal the things that guide your thoughts and frame your view. I'm going to do this because, whatever your view – however you see things – they make up the window through which you look.

In part two, I'm going to go farther. I'm going to talk about critical thinking, and offer some practical advice on how to think critically in the real world. I'm not going to offer a set of rules to help you get it *right*. I don't claim to know the *truth*. I'm a Professor of History and Theory of Psychology at the University of Edinburgh, where I've taught critical thinking, and have also written about its history. This is what I know.

Throughout the history of thinking – both critical and uncritical thinking – our views have been quietly shaped by things that we rarely, if ever, notice. They're out of sight, and they remain out of sight, because they're in the ways that we look. So, to make more sense of the world, a more radical way is needed. We need to remind ourselves that thinking is a process, not an outcome. It's a path that can lead to different conclusions.

This is a curious walk along that path. If you walk this way, then I hope, at the end of the road, you'll be able to make better sense of it all.

If you're still curious, we can start from here.

The front door of 23 George Square

I

What we notice

SHERLOCK HOLMES: *You see but you do not observe. The distinction is clear. For example, you have frequently seen the steps which lead up from the hall to this room.*
DR WATSON: *Frequently.*
HOLMES: *How often?*
WATSON: *Well, some hundreds of times.*
HOLMES: *Then how many are there?*
WATSON: *How many? I don't know.*
HOLMES: *Quite so! You have not observed. And yet you have seen.*[1]

I'm in my office. It's in the Department of Psychology, which is on George Square. I'm feeling more like Watson than Holmes. However, as we'll see, I think that this is a good thing.

There's a stairway nearby, which leads down to the ground floor. It also leads up from the ground floor to here. This, as the comedian Chic Murray used to say, saves us from needing two stairways. I've gone up and down these stairs ... well, some hundreds of times. However, I've never observed how many steps there are.

Radical Thinking

Like Watson, even the things that we see, we frequently fail to notice. For example, you just read the last sentence, but you didn't notice how many words were there. Perhaps you just went back to count them. We notice things after they're brought to our attention. That's when they become relevant. But we can't notice everything. So, we filter. We select, out of everything that we can see, what seems relevant and what doesn't. And, when you're reading, the number of words in a sentence is irrelevant. That's why, when you read the last sentence, you didn't notice how many words were there.

There's nothing wrong with that but, when we're told this, it can sound like a criticism. That's how Sherlock Holmes talks to Watson, who, in the original books, is the reader's eyes and ears on what the great detective is thinking. Holmes observes all. Watson doesn't. And we, the reader, feel like Watson, who, compared to Holmes, has inadequate eyes and ears.

We've been told a similar story by psychologists. For over a century, they've pointed out how little we notice and how inaccurately we see and hear things. Our eyes and ears are prone to deception. We fail to notice what stares us in the face. Our memories are unreliable. Our thoughts are irrational. If we hear this, then it might make us feel inadequate. But compared to what exactly?

It's easy to point to our imperfections, because we have so many, but we're not supposed to be perfect. We're humans, whose eyes are not cameras and whose minds are not computers, though we invented both. After we invented them, they became metaphors for how we see, and how we think.[2] However, when we compare ourselves to our inventions, we often suffer by comparison. And, when we compare ourselves to invented characters, such as Sherlock

Holmes, who is more observant than us – but who is fictional – we suffer by comparison.

We'll never notice everything because we need to focus on some things, not others. We can't see things as they really are, or think in merely rational ways, because we're neither cameras nor computers. We can't be truly objective because we see things from our current position. These are our natural limits. When they're pointed out, of course, we take notice. And then we carry on as normal, not noticing how many steps are there. Or how many words were in the last sentence.

The basic point is this: the problem of thinking in the real world isn't that we're inadequate, but that we forget our limits. We notice a limited number of things and interpret these things in a particular way. This is the window through which we look at the world: everything that we think is based on what we notice and on how we interpret it. Beyond this, there are all the things that we miss, and there are alternative interpretations. This is the bigger picture.

In the real world, we have natural limits, and it's useful to be reminded of them, not because we should have superhuman powers but because, as humans, we don't.

Holmes, of course, was a fictional character. However, the human who invented him was real. And Arthur Conan Doyle was no Sherlock Holmes.

Indeed, as we'll see, he's a useful reminder of our limits.

It took a couple of minutes to walk from my office to 23 George Square. I've walked past this doorway hundreds of times but, until now, I've never noticed that, in front of the doorway, there are four steps. So, when you glanced at the photograph at the start of this

Radical Thinking

chapter, you probably didn't notice this either (though, now that I've made this relevant, perhaps you just went back to count them). The reason that 23 George Square is relevant is this: it's where Arthur Conan Doyle lived.

Doyle was here while he was a student. In 1876, he began to study medicine at the University of Edinburgh and then at the Extra-Mural School of Medicine. He took a course on clinical surgery, which was taught by the surgeon Joseph Bell. Bell was famous for his powers of observation in the diagnosis of patients. He became the inspiration for Sherlock Holmes.

Doyle wrote to him later: 'It is most certainly to you that I owe Sherlock Holmes … I do not think his analytical work is in the least an exaggeration of some of the effects which I have seen you produce in the out-patient ward.'[3]

Doyle recalled an example of Bell's powers of deduction, based on close observation:

> At an out-patient clinic, a patient is shown in. Before the patient can say a word, Bell says:
>
> 'Well, my man, I see you've served in the army.'
>
> 'Aye sir.'
>
> 'Not long discharged?'
>
> 'Aye sir.'
>
> 'A Highland regiment?'
>
> 'Aye sir.'
>
> 'A non-commissioned officer?'
>
> 'Aye sir.'
>
> 'Stationed at Barbados?'
>
> 'Aye sir.'

Bell then explained to Doyle and his fellow students how he'd done it:

> 'You see, gentlemen, the patient is a respectful man but he did not remove his hat. They do not do this in the army. He would have learned this civilian habit had he been long discharged. He has an air of authority and he is obviously Scottish. As to Barbados, his complaint is elephantiasis which is West Indian and not British.'[4]

A few years later, Sherlock Holmes would be demonstrating similar powers of deduction, based on close observation, by noticing relevant facts and then interpreting them in a certain way. However, according to an old friend, Bell described these stories as 'drivel'.[5] He thought that they exaggerated the limits of his powers. 'From close observation and deduction, gentlemen, it is possible to make a diagnosis that will be correct in any and every case,' Bell admitted, but he stressed that 'you must not neglect to ratify your deductions [and] substantiate your diagnosis'.[6] He would often tell his students of one occasion when he'd visited a patient.

He'd quickly deduced that the patient was a bandsman. He explained to his students at the time: 'You see, gentlemen, I am right. It is quite simple. This man has paralysis of the cheek muscles, the result of too much blowing at wind instruments.' Bell then asked which instrument the patient played, and the man replied: 'The big drum.'[7]

Bell told this story to make it clear: he understood the limits of his powers.

Doyle, however, wasn't so aware. For example, he observed many spiritualist mediums. He observed them closely and took copious notes. He observed fraud in some cases. He didn't observe it in most. He deduced, therefore, that most mediums were genuine.[8] In other words, he assumed that, if he didn't observe fraud, then it wasn't there. As he once told the legendary magician (and well-known sceptic) Harry Houdini: 'I am a cool observer and do not make mistakes.'[9]

Doyle also observed Houdini and deduced some things about him. He observed Houdini with his own eyes, and he read the accounts of Houdini's performances. He deduced that Houdini was able to pass through solid obstacles by dematerialising and reassembling his body. He was aware that Houdini was a magician and that it might be a trick. He observed that there were tricks in which magicians escaped from boxes, bags and handcuffs. He read how they were done. But he deduced that Houdini's performances were different and that *his* relied on psychic powers. He was perfectly aware that Houdini denied this. Houdini and Doyle were friends for years and Houdini told him directly, more than once, that he had no psychic powers. But Doyle didn't accept the denials. He deduced that, like others before him, Houdini was reluctant to admit his psychic powers.[10]

What Doyle thought was based on what he saw and heard (with his own eyes and ears), which he then interpreted in a particular way. That's what we all do, though what we notice and how we interpret it is often very different. For example, having read what Doyle observed and how he interpreted it, you might think that he was wrong. You might think that the mediums were fake, and that Doyle failed to notice this. You might think that, when Houdini said that he had no psychic powers, he was telling the truth.

That's what I think, though how we interpret what we see and hear tends to be in line with what we believe. Like Doyle, my beliefs are based on my experience, but my experience has been different. Naturally, I wasn't there at the séances that Doyle attended. However, I've read hundreds of séance accounts from the Victorian period, and I know how mediums were able to fake it. I'm sure that many of them did, though I can't be certain that all of them did. And, as a historian of magic, I know how Houdini performed his escapes.

So, it seems clear to me that Doyle forgot his limits. He thought that he was 'a cool observer [who did] not make mistakes'. He'd created a fictional character who miraculously observed all that he saw. In the real world, however, you can't observe everything that you see. You can't observe anything without interpreting it. And you can't observe what you don't see.

Doyle was Watson but thought that he was Holmes. He didn't realise how much he was missing. And neither do we. We need to keep that in mind.

That's why, when I feel like Watson, not Holmes, I think that this is a good thing.

So, what was he missing? What are *we* missing?

I'm now back in the Department of Psychology. From the window upstairs, I can see the back of the Edinburgh Festival Theatre. It's on the site of the old Empire Palace Theatre, once the largest theatre in Britain. When Houdini came to Edinburgh in 1914, that was where he performed. The *Scotsman* newspaper curiously observed that his act, 'though not new to Edinburgh audiences, [was] if anything more interesting and mystifying at the second time of seeing'.[11] They still couldn't see what they were missing.

Magicians have performed in Edinburgh for centuries. They performed on the streets of the Old Town and in the assembly rooms of the New Town. Throughout this time, they made a living by exploiting how much we miss. With bold gestures and flamboyant patter, they distracted observers' eyes and ears. However, by the time that Houdini was performing in large theatres, magicians had got even better at controlling what the audience noticed. They'd started to use 'misdirection' to mislead not only their audiences' eyes and ears, but also their audiences' minds.[12] If you can misdirect the minds of observers, then you can direct not only what they notice, but also how they interpret what they see. The man who inspired Houdini – the French magician Robert-Houdin – had explained how this could be done.

One way was to present things so that they seemed ordinary and natural. No more bold gestures and flamboyant patter. These attracted attention and distracted the audience, but they did so in an obvious way. They were out of the ordinary and, as a result, they immediately aroused suspicion. The audience might not see what was going on, but they knew that they were being distracted. They knew that they were missing *something*. A better way to deceive the audience, according to Robert-Houdin, was to speak and act in natural ways.[13] That way, the audience would feel that they were seeing all that there was to see.

Another way to misdirect the minds of the audience, he explained, was to suggest that what was going on was actually something else. If it was done by sleight of hand, for example, then it should be presented as technology. If it relied on a mechanical device, then it should be presented as sleight of hand.[14] After all, the audience knew that there was a secret. They were looking for what they were missing. However, by directing their attention to this not that, the audience would think about this not that, which would send not only their eyes, but also their minds, in the wrong direction.

These techniques were revealed in popular books.[15] These books were read by the public, who went to see magic shows, but they still didn't see what was going on. When people are told what they're missing, they first take notice, but then they carry on as normal. Not noticing how many words were in the last sentence. Houdini read these books, and he learned the techniques. He used them when he performed magic and when he presented his famous escapes. He also knew how spiritualist mediums, like the ones who convinced Arthur Conan Doyle, might use similar techniques.[16]

We can't be certain what Doyle was missing, but we can be sure that these techniques worked, because they were used by many fraudulent mediums. For example, when mediums conducted séances, they normally did so in the dark. This made it hard to notice what was going on, which initially aroused suspicion. However, mediums spoke of the need for darkness, of the sensitivity of the phenomena to light, and compared it all to the development of a photograph. This made the darkness seem natural.

Spiritualists who visited these mediums knew that it might be a trick and often attempted to prevent fraud. But mediums claimed that the phenomena could only be produced in certain conditions and that a sceptical attitude wasn't helpful. This became an accepted norm in spiritualist circles. Like darkness, it came to be seen as natural. As Doyle said himself: 'you must submit in a humble spirit to psychic conditions.'[17]

Mediums also had to present what they did as the work of the spirits. After all, there was little about what people saw and heard that was obviously 'spiritual'. They saw tables move and heard knocking noises. They saw words appear on blank slates. They heard the voice of the medium. But mediums presented these movements and messages as physical manifestations of the spirits. They presented themselves as mere conduits of the spirits: the medium had no control, it took great effort, and success couldn't be guaranteed. If nothing happened, then it wasn't their fault. But if something happened, then they could all be thankful that the spirits had decided to attend. This focused attention on the spirits, not the medium.[18]

By creating conditions that seemed natural, and by attributing what they did to a different cause, mediums (at least the fraudulent ones) prevented observers from seeing what was really going on. They also provided a way for them to *interpret* what they saw. After all, in the case of a magic trick, if you can't see how it's done, then you deduce that it's a good trick. When Doyle observed mediums, he couldn't see how it was done. He deduced, therefore, that it was real. In the process, he forgot his limits, which led him to think that, if he didn't see it, then it wasn't there. He thought that he'd seen things as they really were.

But Doyle was simply doing what we all do, one way or another, most of the time. Magicians and fraudulent mediums were simply exploiting the ways that we look at the world and, in the process, how much we miss.

What we miss, and what we observe, depends on a variety of things. We notice the obvious, like a loud noise, a sudden movement or a flashing light. We notice things that are **bold** and *flamboyant*. But we're aware that these have grabbed our attention. We tend not to notice what seems ordinary or natural. We notice what seems novel or out of place. That, however, depends on the surroundings.

What we notice

This seems novel, but novelties wear off. After a while, once we've adjusted to the new conditions, this now seems novel.

What first seems novel begins to seem natural. We quickly become accustomed to the dark. As we do, we forget how little we see.

Our attention is directed by expectations. We look where we anticipate that something is going to happen ... something is going to happen ... something is going to ... even if it doesn't. We notice what we think is currently relevant because, in that moment, it matters. When we're crossing the road, we observe the traffic and don't see the pedestrians on the pavements. When watching a magician shuffle the cards, we observe the cards, the hands, the movement, but not the box on the table nearby. When attending a séance, spiritualists might initially watch the medium, but then they look for evidence of the spirits, because that's why they're there. When reading a book, we pay attention to what the words mean, not to how many are there. And, of course, as we stare at our phones, the real world passes us by. This is how we look at the world: we pay attention to what we think matters and miss what else is going on.

Psychologists have conducted various experiments to show how little we observe. In what's probably now the most famous experiment, subjects were shown a video clip of two teams playing basketball. They were asked to count the number of passes made by the team in white – *not* the team in black. Meanwhile, a person in a gorilla suit wandered through the game. Yet most of the subjects didn't notice this.[19] This video has since been shown to countless groups as an example of how much we fail to observe (what psychologists call 'inattentional blindness'). It's made people wonder how they could fail to spot something as obvious as a gorilla. It's a useful

Radical Thinking

reminder of our limits. However, it needn't make us feel inadequate. After all, nobody failed to spot a gorilla. There was no gorilla in the video.

There was a person wearing a gorilla suit, who walked like a human being. She was surrounded by others who were also dressed in black outfits – while observers were trying to ignore people who were dressed in black outfits. If there had been a real gorilla, then *that* would have been obvious. It would have moved in very different ways, and the basketball game would have ended abruptly. Most observers failed to spot the person in a gorilla suit because it wasn't relevant. They were focusing on the task that they'd been given, which demanded their full attention. They would have also failed to spot the shoes that the psychologist was wearing. Or how many words were in the last sentence.

There are countless things that we fail to observe, but our limits, in terms of what we notice, are finite. They depend on where we direct our attention. That, in turn, depends on what, in any given context, we think is relevant. At the end of the day, that's up to us. However, when our attention is directed by others, we see what they want us to see, and we fail to notice the bigger picture. This has been demonstrated by magicians and psychologists.

It has also been exploited by politicians. They make bold gestures and flamboyant announcements to direct our attention to this not that. We may be suspicious, but we nevertheless look. They make some things relevant, so that we think about *those* things. They send our minds in the wrong direction. They do it so often that it seems natural, and we fail to notice what's going on. We become accustomed to the dark and soon forget how little we see. They help us to forget how much we're missing until we think that we're seeing all there is. We see things the way that they want us to see them, because they provide a window through which we can view things on their terms. As a result, it seems as if there's nothing else, and no alternative view.

But there is. We just need to remember our limits. We notice only a fraction of what's out there. Whatever we notice, we always interpret it in a particular way. However, if we direct our attention elsewhere, then we'll see other things. And, as we'll see later, if we take the time to consider alternative perspectives, then we'll see things differently.

Meanwhile, when we think about how much we miss, it's easy to miss the less obvious thing: how much we manage to see. We see faces in clouds, ghosts in shadows, meaning in inkblots and order in chaos. We see things that aren't really there.

I learned this in Edinburgh. I was raised here as a Catholic and, as a child, I was taught the doctrine of transubstantiation. During the part of the Mass called the Eucharist, bread transforms into the flesh of Christ, yet the bread continues to look like bread, feel like bread, and taste like bread. This isn't supposed to be a metaphor but a literal transformation of ordinary bread into the body of Christ. Nevertheless, according to the senses, nothing changes. It is, quite literally, non-sense. As a child, I didn't understand this non-sense and so I asked my teacher. However, he didn't understand it either and so I asked the priest. He explained that we don't see things as they really are. We need to rely on faith.

At about the same time, in a completely unrelated context, a woman in New Mexico noticed the face of Jesus on a tortilla.[20] She decided not to eat the tortilla. Instead, she called a priest. The priest was sceptical. Nevertheless, the tortilla was framed, placed in a shrine, and attracted countless pilgrims. They waited in line, with the patience that comes of faith, to witness the miraculous breadstuff. It became international news, with photographs of the tortilla appearing in newspapers all over the world, so that others could judge for themselves. Since then, the face of Jesus has appeared on pancakes, poppadoms and pizzas. It's been found on a tree stump. It's been discovered inside the lid of a jar of Marmite. It's been spotted on a wood panel of a toilet door in the Glasgow branch of IKEA. And this is only part of the miracle because, every time that Jesus has appeared, his face has mysteriously changed. Nevertheless, the faithful have been able to see, in these vague yet noticeably different markings, the face of Jesus.

Can you see the face of Jesus? For an alternative interpretation, compare it to the photo on the back cover of the book.

What we notice

At about the same time, in a completely unrelated context, Woody Allen wrote a profound sentence about a mythical beast: it had the body of a lion, and the head of a lion, though not of the same lion.[21] After I read this sentence, I visited Edinburgh Zoo and looked at a lion. I looked at the lion for quite some time, until I managed to convince myself, just for a moment, that it was the mythical beast. In that briefest of moments, as I looked at the lion and imagined that it was more than I could see, I finally understood the power of faith to shape how we interpret the world. It was only a brief moment, however, because I then remembered that Woody Allen had been joking.

Faith is a magical window through which the mundane can be transformed into something extraordinary. But we all have faith of one kind or another, because faith takes many forms. We don't see the world as it really is. We see it through a window that's loyal to certain assumptions about what there is, and to certain expectations about what will be. This can lead us to notice things that aren't really there. A missing key. The emptiness of a wallet. A train that hasn't arrived yet.

Whatever is really out there, we notice this not that, and we interpret it as 'this' not 'that'. We itnerpert waht we see in trems taht we can udnersatnd. We tarnsfrom waht is out terhe itno semothnig taht mkaes snese to us. In the porcses, we can see the fcae of Jseus – even though it's not really there.

To make more sense of the world, then, we need to be more curious about what we're missing, and about how we interpret what we see. We needn't be a Sherlock Holmes to see that what we notice, and what we miss, depends on where we direct our attention. This is guided by what we think matters. We needn't see the body of Christ,

35

Radical Thinking

the face of Jesus, or a mythical beast, to realise that, whatever we happen to see, we interpret it in a particular way. This is shaped by what we take for granted, what we believe, and what we want.

This is the window through which we look at the world, and it limits our view. If we wish to see the bigger picture, then we need to think in a more radical way. We need to look farther than what seems obvious.

So, having returned from Arthur Conan Doyle's former home, on the west side of George Square, it's time to look elsewhere.

2

A limited picture

I'm now on the east side of George Square, looking eastwards. From here, I can see Nicolson Street. That's where it began.

In the summer of 1777, the son of a baker and the son of a wigmaker decided to publish a book.[1] It would be an extraordinarily large book: it would cover 'the whole field of human knowledge'.[2] It took seven years to publish the whole thing. The book first appeared in a printing shop on Nicolson Street owned by the wigmaker's son.[3] It was called *Encyclopaedia Britannica*.

It was an attempt to describe the biggest of pictures. However, it presented a picture of the world that was remarkably incomplete. It was limited in much the same ways that our own views of the world are limited. Indeed, it's a lesson in why, no matter how comprehensive our world-view might seem to be, we need to look farther.

It wasn't the first encyclopaedia. It wasn't even the first *Encyclopaedia Britannica*. They'd published the first edition of *Britannica* a few years earlier. However, that had been a far more modest affair: just three volumes and not particularly original. One reviewer had dismissed it as a work that had been 'ignorantly, and, upon the whole,

Radical Thinking

we may add, dishonestly, executed'.[4] It was also rather limited in scope. It didn't include history. It didn't include biographies.

But the second edition, which began to appear in 1777, was much more ambitious. This 'greatly improved and enlarged' edition covered all the usual things: 'the different sciences and arts' and 'all the countries, cities, principal mountains, seas, rivers, etc. throughout the world'. It covered 'matters ecclesiastical, civil, military, commercial, etc.' However, this edition also included history and biographies. It boasted 'a general history, ancient and modern, of the different empires, kingdoms and states'. It included 'an account of the lives of all the most eminent persons of every nation'.[5] It also featured over 300 copperplate engravings. The first instalment, which included Aberdeen, Aborigines, Abortion and Abraham, cost a shilling.

By 1784, all 181 instalments had been bound into ten large volumes. The fifth volume (G–H) included the new article on 'History'. It was written by Adam Ferguson, one of the great intellectuals of the Enlightenment. Ferguson was a philosopher at the University of Edinburgh. He was a friend of David Hume and Adam Smith. He has been described as the 'father of Sociology'.[6] The two great Scottish writers, Robert Burns and Walter Scott, met only once and, when they met, it was at the house of Adam Ferguson.[7]

Ferguson's article on 'History' provided 'an account of the principal transactions of mankind since the beginning of the world'.[8] In just forty-four pages. According to one of the great intellectuals of the Enlightenment, the history of the world went something like this:

It began around 4000 BC. That was when God created the earth (according to studies of the Old Testament). During the early period, 'men were not at that time in a savage state' and 'lived in one vast community'. After 1,656 years, however, they 'had proceeded to

A limited picture

greater and greater lengths of wickedness'. At that point, 'the Deity thought proper to send a flood on the earth, which destroyed the whole human race except eight persons.' These eight persons (i.e. 'Noah and his family'), accompanied by the animals that they'd saved on the Ark, began to repopulate the world with their many and various offspring. A few centuries later, when most of the human race was assembled in Babylonia, they decided to build the Tower of Babel, which 'gave offence to the Deity'. His punishment was to create a variety of languages, which divided mankind into different nations.[9]

The civil history of the world continued. The sons of Noah and their various offspring settled in different parts of the world, kept largely to themselves and acquired different characters, some 'more civilized' and 'others more barbarous'. Kingdoms arose in Babylonia, Assyria and Egypt, and in rather less civilised places such as Sodom and Gomorrah. It continued with the establishment of the Greek city states, the rise and fall of Rome, and a host of other lesser empires. Religious history, from the Garden of Eden to the Reformation, focused on the 'true religion', the power of pretentious popes in the West, the 'absurd doctrines of Mahomet' in the East, and the persistence of these and other uncivilised superstitions. The article ended with a lengthy essay about the nature of history, which discussed what should and shouldn't be included. After all, as Ferguson pointed out: 'all facts do not merit the regard of an historian.'[10]

What to include? This has always been a problem for the historian. It was a significantly larger problem for the compilers of the encyclopaedia. The second edition of *Britannica* was, at the time, the largest encyclopaedia in the English language. However, it couldn't include everything. Though it did include over 300 copperplate engravings. Twenty-four of these engravings appeared in the entry for 'War'. The full article on 'War' spanned a remarkable 184 pages (the history of the world had been covered in forty-four). However, there was no entry for 'Peace'.

If you explore the fifth volume (G–H) further, then you discover something else that's curious. It provides some context for Ferguson's article on 'History'. If you turn back from the H's to the G's, then you realise that something is missing. The article on 'Geography' ends on page 3368. The next entry is 'Geometry'. In a book intended to cover 'the whole field of human knowledge', there was no entry for 'Geology'.

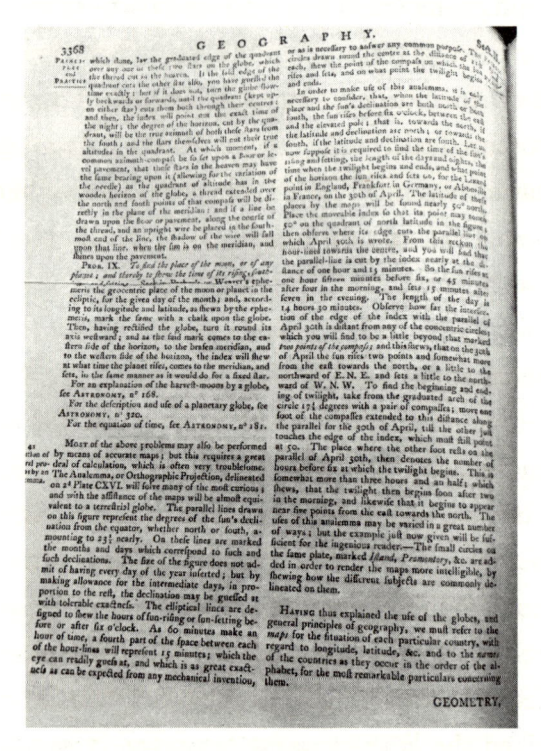

From the second edition of *Britannica*, which attempted to cover the whole of human knowledge, but nobody noticed that there was something missing.

They could not, of course, include the *whole* of human knowledge. So, what was included, and what was missing, was based on a number of criteria. Some of the content was *obvious*. It had been included in earlier encyclopaedias. Some of it was easily *available*. The publishers copied verbatim from other works (to the extent that this resulted in a lawsuit).[11] They didn't include 'Geology' because that wasn't available (at that time, there was no subject of Geology).

Some of the content was designed to be *appealing*. They included a new article on 'Legerdemain' that described a selection of the best magic tricks and explained how they were done. They included over 300 copperplate engravings. And, whatever was included, it had to seem *relevant* to their customers. In the opening preface, they assured the potential customer – a Christian man who could afford to buy it – that he was inclined 'to culture and refinement to a very high degree', and that the cultivation of such knowledge was 'not only conducive, but essential, to his happiness'.[12]

They included what was obvious and available. They included what would seem appealing and relevant.

The new biographies included people who had 'excelled in the arts of war and peace, or such as have either distinguished themselves in the theatre of action or in the recess of contemplation'.[13] They included those who were considered eminent: monarchs and generals, aristocrats and saints. They didn't include the ordinary folk who had fought in wars for monarchs and generals, and who had died in the theatre of action. They didn't include the ordinary folk who had worked the land for aristocrats, and who had prayed to the saints for something better. They excluded the vast majority of people. There were, for example, no bakers or wigmakers.

Radical Thinking

A woman might make an occasional appearance, if she was a monarch, an aristocrat or a saint. There was, however, an entry for 'Lady', which observed that the word could now be used to describe 'all eminent women'. The origin of the word, it explained, was a contraction of *loaf-day*, from a time when a female member of one of 'those families, whom God had blessed with affluence … distributed to her poor neighbours, *with her own hands* [original italics], a certain quantity of bread'. It was suggested that this may be why 'to this day, the ladies in this kingdom alone serve the meat at their own tables'.[14] The entry for 'Woman' was significantly briefer: 'the female of the human species'.[15]

By the standards of the day, there was nothing surprising. Before the emergence of Geology, the Bible story was considered to be true by virtually everyone who read the encyclopaedia. The date of Creation, according to the King James Bible, was 4004 BC. If the Bible story was true, then the dates of Creation and The Flood, and the origins of different languages and nations, all made sense. This, at the time, seemed *obvious*. It was based on what, at the time, was *available*.

Of course, nobody read the whole thing. The encyclopaedia was something to own, to display on the shelves and occasionally to peruse – though one would imagine that many were attracted to a history of the world in forty-four pages. They read the parts that they found *appealing*. They read the parts that they thought were *relevant*. They ignored the vast majority of it. Nevertheless, the very presence on the shelves of a set of volumes containing 'the whole of human knowledge' must have been a comforting thought.

This is what an encyclopaedia does. It gives the illusion of completeness. It's what a history of the world does. It has the appearance of the whole. However, it's only a fraction of the whole. And it's not a random selection.

Your experience of the world is similar.

It has the appearance of the whole. However, it's only a fraction of what's out there. It's limited to what seems obvious and what's available. It's shaped by what you find appealing and what you think is relevant.

You notice what seems obvious. It's staring you in the face – it's right here – so, you can't miss it. You notice what's available. It requires little effort – the local environment, the daily routine, the usual suspects – so, it's hard to avoid. You're drawn to what's appealing. It's what you prefer and what others admire – the top ten, five-star reviews, the best deal – so, you're attracted to it. You take an interest in what seems relevant. It's in the air and on your radar – today's headlines, this week's meme, the flavour of the month, the event of the year – so, it gets your attention. Meanwhile, you don't see what's out of sight and, therefore, out of mind. You avoid those things that don't appeal and ignore what you think doesn't matter.

Wherever we happen to be, we see and hear a fraction of what's going on. If we wish to get a sense of perspective, then we need to think about what we're missing. To see the bigger picture, we need to look farther. But where to look? After all, the sources of what we see and hear have changed. For most of history, we relied on our own eyes and ears, and those of the people we encountered. In recent centuries, we've relied on newspapers to provide us with a daily view of the world.

A newspaper is a history of yesterday. It presents a particular picture, one that's framed by the views and interests of the editor.

Radical Thinking

It may be the truth, but it's never the whole truth. It includes some things and leaves out others, and what's included is always interpreted in a particular way. If we take the time to compare different newspapers, however, then we can spot the differences. We can appreciate different perspectives.

Now and again, we're given a range of views, but that's normally because our attention is directed towards a single thing. A national vote. A controversial tweet. A global crisis. The most recent meme. It's covered from countless different viewpoints, and every new angle is explored because novelty gets our attention. But what's new isn't necessarily important. Everyone has a voice, but not all voices are deep, and some are more flamboyant than others. Amid the noise, the endless variations on a theme can saturate our eyes and ears, until all we can see or hear is the most recent take on the only thing that appears to matter. With so many views on a single thing, it's easy to lose sight of the bigger picture. However, we can always skip the front page and direct our attention to less obvious matters, which continue to be relevant beyond the headlines.

I was thinking about this in the middle of September 2022, when the headlines were all about the death of the Queen. She had died a week earlier. She was ninety-six years old. I was thinking about this because, at the time, it had been on the front page of every newspaper, and had dominated every news programme, every day since. However, a week earlier, fifteen thousand children had also died. They were under five years old. And this had happened every day since. But this hadn't been news. It happened every day.[16] And it's still happening. It's largely a result of poverty and attracts less attention. From here, it's not obvious. It doesn't seem relevant.

A limited picture

I don't know what, on the day that you read this, the number will be. However, it's not novel, so it won't be news.

Today, of course, we get our news through a screen. This is now the window through which we look at the world, since it's so easily available. However, it limits what we notice because, as it provides us with information, it also gets information from us. It uses that information to feed us what we want to hear, and to offer us things that we might want to buy. It shows us things that we'll find appealing. It uses algorithms that direct our attention to this not that. It appears to offer greater diversity but, to the individual, it offers less. And, in this vast connected world, we feel more individual than ever.

We're increasingly isolated, like brains in a vat, who depend on electronic lifelines for support. They link us up to an artificial community of folk who like each other's thoughts. They tie us to an endless series of posts that reinforce each other, which create a sense of security, one from which it's hard to escape. We keep our heads down, for fear of heckling from anonymous strangers who condemn without thought, or who stir things up to gain attention, which limits what we can say out loud. We restrict ourselves to virtual friends, with whom we share cherry-picked images of ourselves, which present a veneer – an illusion of solidity and depth – which is only convincing from a distance.

No touching, no scratching the surface, no *real* interaction that might make us vulnerable to detection. Behind our respective screens, we hide from scrutiny and wish we were as smart and happy as the selves that we present online. Within this world, we feel important because we've wrapped and trapped ourselves in a comfortable blanket of synthetic material, which keeps us insulated, but

Radical Thinking

also isolated, from the real world beyond the closed circuit. We see a fraction of what's out there, and we project a fraction of who we are.

However, if we put our real selves out there, with all our limits, then we might discover what we really think, who we really are, and what we're missing. If we look farther – beyond the closed circuit – then we'll notice other things. They may seem strange and unexpected. They may not fit with our existing world-view. We may discover that our view was too limited and we might be inclined to change our minds. We'll certainly discover that we're not the centre of the universe.

That may change how we look at the world and how we see ourselves.

I'm still on the east side of George Square, looking eastwards. However, looking *farther* – beyond Nicolson Street – I can see the Radical Road.

It winds its way round Salisbury Crags, the domineering cliff that gently descends towards the extinct volcano known as Arthur's Seat. This is where, as the second edition of *Encyclopaedia Britannica* was still being completed, something else began.

At the time, James Hutton was studying rock formations in Salisbury Crags. While he was there, he noticed something that nobody else had noticed. Later, in the spring of 1785, he presented a paper to the Royal Society of Edinburgh. In this paper, Hutton explained that he'd discovered a junction between different kinds of rock, which must have been formed at different times and in different ways. This was the origin of Geology.

Hutton deduced, on the basis of his observations, that the earth was much older than the Bible suggested. However, this wasn't obvious. The composition of rock revealed a process so slow and gradual that it was invisible to the human eye. It revealed a hidden process with 'no vestige of a beginning [and] no prospect of an end'.[17] To those who assumed that God had created the world in 4004 BC, this was a radical claim. And, at the time, some people thought that he'd gone too far.

Over the following decades, however, Hutton's theories were promoted by John Playfair, a professor of Mathematics at the university, and were later popularised by Charles Lyell in his book *Principles of Geology* (1830–33). By then, Charles Darwin had visited Salisbury Crags to see the rock formations with his own eyes. But when he read Lyell's book, it changed how he looked at the world. He said that 'it altered the whole tone of one's mind' and 'that when seeing a thing never seen by Lyell, one yet saw it partially through his eyes'.[18]

Darwin became a protégé of Lyell. Theories of gradual evolution emerged and these gradually evolved over time. Since then, we've looked farther back. We've learned that the earth is millions of years old and that humans evolved over hundreds of thousands of years. Hutton's exploration of Salisbury Crags, just beyond where *Britannica* began, was the start of that profound shift in how we look at the world and ourselves.

However, for this shift to happen, something else extraordinary had to happen: we had to change our minds. We had to question the truth of the Bible. We had to be persuaded by the evidence – and to embrace the new perspective that it offered – to come to the conclusion that God did *not* create the world, including us, around 4000 BC. We had to *reinterpret* fossils – which had been thought to be animal remains of the Flood – as evidence of much earlier life.

Radical Thinking

This didn't happen immediately, of course, and it wasn't a universal conversion. Some didn't wish to look any farther than the familiar Bible story. They tried to ignore the new evidence and, as it was made increasingly obvious, they chose to interpret it differently. One response, which appeared around the time of Darwin's *On the Origin of Species* (1859), was this: fossils were created by God, along with everything else, around 4000 BC. They were created by God to make the world *appear* to be older than it was. He'd done this to test our faith.[19]

This was an interesting argument, which provided a lifeline to the faithful, who were beginning to drown in the facts. If it were true, then geological findings and evolutionary theories could be ignored. After all, they depended on evidence, and all the evidence could be explained away: it had all been created by God around 4000 BC. Because the Bible told them so. It wasn't a very popular theory, however, even among the faithful. The very idea that God would try to deceive us in such a way wasn't appealing. Surely He wouldn't do that sort of thing.

Nevertheless, the argument survived – it also evolved – and there are now many versions of it. The problem with such an argument is this: we can't disprove it. The world *might* have been created more recently – say, sixteen seconds ago – including all our personal memories and every piece of historical evidence that points to a considerably longer past. There's no evidence that can disprove this: any piece of evidence that we find can be interpreted as having been created only sixteen seconds ago.[20]

The problem with this theory is that, if no evidence can show it to be false, then it's an unfalsifiable theory. This makes it unscientific. However, it doesn't make it untrue. Perhaps God *did* create the

A limited picture

world, including all the evidence that He didn't, sixteen seconds ago. Perhaps there are secret rulers of the world, though nobody has seen them, because they're invisible. Perhaps there's a vast conspiracy, though there's no evidence because 'they' have covered it up. Such things are possible but, without any evidence, we have no reason to believe them. There's only an unshifting faith in a way of thinking that needs no evidence. This is the point of departure, from which the path leads in only one direction. It's a belief so fundamental that, no matter what evidence is encountered, it can't be altered. In other words, it's fundamentalism.

Fundamentalism ties its followers to a series of assertions that reinforce each other, which create a sense of security, but one from which it's hard to escape. It presents a veneer – an illusion of solidity and depth – which is only convincing from a distance. No scratching the surface, no deeper scrutiny which might make its flaws vulnerable to detection. It appeals to people by offering a sense of certainty and by telling them that they're important. However, it does this by ignoring anything that questions it, which is a position of ignorance. It wraps them in a comfortable blanket of synthetic material, which keeps them insulated from the real world beyond the closed circuit.

We need to look farther to get beyond it. We need to look beyond the fundamentals, beyond the things that we take for granted – we need to think in a radical way – to see the bigger picture.

We may, as individuals, notice only a fraction of what's going on. However, as humans, our combined observations add up to so much more. Since Hutton, countless experts have examined the evidence and have explored new theories by asking new questions, making new observations, and then interpreting the evidence in different

Radical Thinking

ways. They've offered a very different perspective than the old one provided by fundamentalists. They've provided a richer and bigger picture. It's one in which *we* aren't so important.

Think of the history of the universe (so far) as if it were a calendar year, i.e. the Big Bang happened on 1 January and the end of the year is today.[21] We humans don't appear until the final day of the final month of the year: on 31 December. Indeed, until eight minutes before midnight. Socrates, Plato, Buddha and Confucius don't appear until *six seconds* before midnight. That's also when we see the appearance of the Old Testament, according to which everything was created by God: just *ten seconds* earlier. That's what we used to think, because the Bible told us so. We used to think that the universe was created sixteen seconds ago.

Since then, most of us have changed our minds. Now we have a sense of perspective: we're not the centre of the universe. The findings of science, of course, don't offer certainty. They offer evidence, which is always limited, so it can't tell the complete story. If you want a sense of certainty, then you need to embrace some kind of fundamentalism, which provides an unchanging story. You need to rely on confident assertions by those who have an immovable faith in (selected parts of) sacred texts, the truth of which is not to be questioned. However, if we remember our limits, and those of the people who pretend to certainty, then we can decide what to think for ourselves.

Any account of the whole of human knowledge – of the history of the universe – of the history of the world – or even of the history of yesterday – is bound to be no more than a fraction of the whole. It focuses our attention on this not that, and presents this in a particular way. In the process, it may provide us with a wider perspective than we can gain from personal experience, but it has its own limits, and it's framed by others. It provides a particular view of the world, based on what they think is obvious and on the information that they have available. It's shaped by what they find appealing and what they think is relevant.

If we wish to find our real place within the bigger picture, then we need to look farther, beyond any *particular* view of the world. As we'll see, we need to consider *alternative* views, which present other content and in different ways. And, if the evidence is better, then we need to be prepared to change our minds. That's how we can see beyond the window through which we currently look.

Meanwhile, I can see the Radical Road from here, which winds its way round Salisbury Crags. If you walk that way, then you can see 'Hutton's Section': a section of rock where Hutton discovered evidence that supported his theory. It suggested a new vision of how the world in which we live was created. Existing landscapes slowly eroded. Rocks and soil were deposited in the sea. Meanwhile, subterranean pressure and heat forced molten rock from the ocean floor up to the earth's surface, creating new mountains and terrains. In this ongoing cycle of death and resurrection, the matter of the world was rearranged. What was once at the bottom of the sea could now be found on the highest land. The oldest rocks that we see are made up of 'materials furnished from the ruins of former continents'.[22]

It was a radical view of transformation, of gradual decay and reconstruction, which was caused by natural decline and growing pressure from below. It was a view of the world that we inhabit as nothing more than the most recent version. Wherever you are in this world, you walk on land that was once foreign. Whatever your current view, from wherever you are, it used to be different and, slowly but surely, it will change.

This change may be imperceptible. Yet Hutton could see it in these rocks on Salisbury Crags. And you can too. However, it's not obvious. You need to interpret the facts so that you understand what they mean. If you do, then from this single spot you can gain a perspective that stretches back so far that you realise your humble place. You're a new arrival in a land in which even the rocks are the result of immigration, and to which you're a fleeting visitor.

From a single position, by looking at things differently, you can discover your place in the world. You're not the centre of the universe. You have a very narrow outlook. It's limited by what seems obvious to you, and by what's available here and now. It's shaped by what you find appealing and what you think is currently relevant. Nevertheless, whatever your position, you can always look at things differently.

Right now, I'm still in the same position, on the east side of George Square, looking eastwards. So, I'm going to turn around. It's time to think about how we interpret what we see.

3

How we interpret things

I'm looking at George Square.

This is how we interpret the world. We look at things and give them names. We use these names, in language and in thought, to represent real things. And, if we share the same language, then we can describe things to each other.

For example, when I tell you that I'm looking at George Square, you understand what I mean. You may not believe that this is true (for example, you might think that, right now, I'm looking at what I'm typing). You may not know what George Square looks like. However, you understand that it's a city square in Edinburgh and that I am (or am not) looking at it.

And this is how you learn about the world beyond your own experience. People have different views of the world. They see certain things and describe them. They claim that this or that is the case. You read or hear these claims, and you believe them. Or, perhaps, you don't. However, before you can accept or reject them, you first need to make sense of them. You need to interpret the claims that they're making. As you do, you tend not to notice the less obvious things that shape your thoughts.

For example, I'm telling you that I can see George Square. However, there's a George Square in Glasgow. If I was there, and I told you that I could see George Square, I'd be talking about something else. And, if you didn't know my position – if you didn't understand the context – then you wouldn't know what I meant.

Interpreting what we see, and what others tell us, is how we make sense of the world in which we live. It's fundamental to everything that we think. As we try to make sense of the world, we come up with names to refer to things. We use them to describe the world. We interpret the world, and we learn about it from others, through the window of language. But the names that we use, and the descriptions of others, have particular meanings. What they mean depends on the context.

The words that we use to refer to things are only useful when we know what they mean. However, this isn't always obvious. When we take them at face value, they quietly shape how we interpret the world. If we're more curious about what they mean, and how they describe the world in a particular way, then we'll notice how they frame the window through which we look.

We use words to represent things. But these things, and the names that we give them, can change. In other words, the link between a name and a thing isn't fixed. What a name means, at any given time and place, will always depend on the context.

For example, I'm looking at George Square. The one in Edinburgh. It was completed in 1785 and it was once Edinburgh's finest suburb. It was originally called 'George's Square'. It was named after George Brown, the brother of the man who designed it.[1] George Brown died in 1806.[2] After that, it was known as 'George Square'.[3]

Same thing. Different name.

George Square was on the southern margin of the city, a tranquil and secluded residence that attracted the most respectable people. Today, however, if you look at a map of Edinburgh, then you'll find George Square in the centre. It's been surpassed and surrounded by more recent developments. It includes newer and taller buildings. It looks very different now. It's still 'George Square', but it's not what it was.

Same name. Different thing.

The tallest building on the square is, from where I'm looking, on my left. It was, until recently, called the David Hume Tower. It was named after the greatest philosopher of the Scottish Enlightenment. Hume wasn't employed as a philosopher by the university, because he was seen as an atheist. Two centuries later, however, they named their tallest building after him, which towers over the nearby church and Edinburgh Central Mosque. But then, in 2020, the context changed again. And so did the name of the building. The university changed the name of the building because of Hume's 'comments on matters of race'.[4]

Since the link between names and things isn't fixed, what names mean depends on the context. And the change in the name of the David Hume Tower is a local example of something larger: the names that we use, and what they mean in a certain context, shape how we interpret things.

For example, Hume made his 'comments on matters of race' in the eighteenth century, so they were hardly new. And anyone who knew Hume's work already knew that he'd made comments that would now be considered racist (though, in his day, the word 'racist' didn't exist). But when you read the views of white men in the eighteenth and nineteenth centuries, you encounter countless references to 'ignorant', 'primitive' and 'inferior' (other) folk. Then and there, that was standard language. Here and now, we dismiss these views as being of their time and place: as ignorant, primitive, and inferior to ours. It's part of our past and, if we know about our past, then we know this.

However, in 2020, in the context of controversies about statues erected to racists and slavers in various cities around the world, this became news. Statues and buildings that had long been passed by, and the names that they represented, were being noticed. This attracted a great deal of controversy. Amid the controversy, however, there was a chance to think more about names and what they represent.

When I first heard that the David Hume Tower had been renamed, this was how I saw it: we knew that he made racist comments, but that's not why the building was named after him. That's not why he mattered. From the perspective of today, Immanuel Kant was a racist and Charles Darwin was a racist. But that's not why they mattered. It was how people thought back then. It was the old normal.

However, now that it had been brought to my attention, I took another look at it. Hume's views weren't simply of their time. They were bad even by the standards of the time. When contemporaries disputed what he said, he persisted. At that time, there were many other places where views about the inferiority of others (for example, Africans) were not the standard (for example, Africa). And, while his racist views may not be why he mattered, they still mattered. They influenced people like Kant and Darwin. They were used, by some, to justify slavery. And we now know that Hume encouraged his patron to buy a slave plantation.[5]

So, the university decided to give the building a new name: 40 George Square. It sounded safe. It sounded neutral. But then it was pointed out that George Brown, the man after whom the square was named, had his own connections to the slave trade. His daughter married into a family whose wealth came from sugar plantations in Jamaica. They owned several hundreds of slaves.[6]

At the time that I write this, I don't know what, at the time that you read this, the name of the building will be. Or even the name of the square. I know where I am, and what I'm looking at, here and now, but that could change. Over time, we see things differently. From David Hume 'the great philosopher', to David Hume 'the racist'. He looks different now. From George Square, once Edinburgh's finest suburb, to George Square, a place named after a man with family connections to the slave trade. I'm still looking at George Square. But it looks different now.

Names, and what they represent to us, matter. They make us see things differently.

Let's consider a slightly bigger picture: Edinburgh. It's had the same name for centuries. However, the city has changed significantly.

In 1750, before George Square was built, the city of Edinburgh was a fish bone. The Castle and the Palace were connected by the High Street, the spine from which dozens of narrow backstreets descended into darker places.

Then Edinburgh decided to improve and branch out. The New Town was designed as a rectangular grid just above the fish bone. It was built on land to the north, but it was designed to express a political view that faced much farther south: the British monarchy and the Union of Scotland and England (which created Great Britain in 1707).

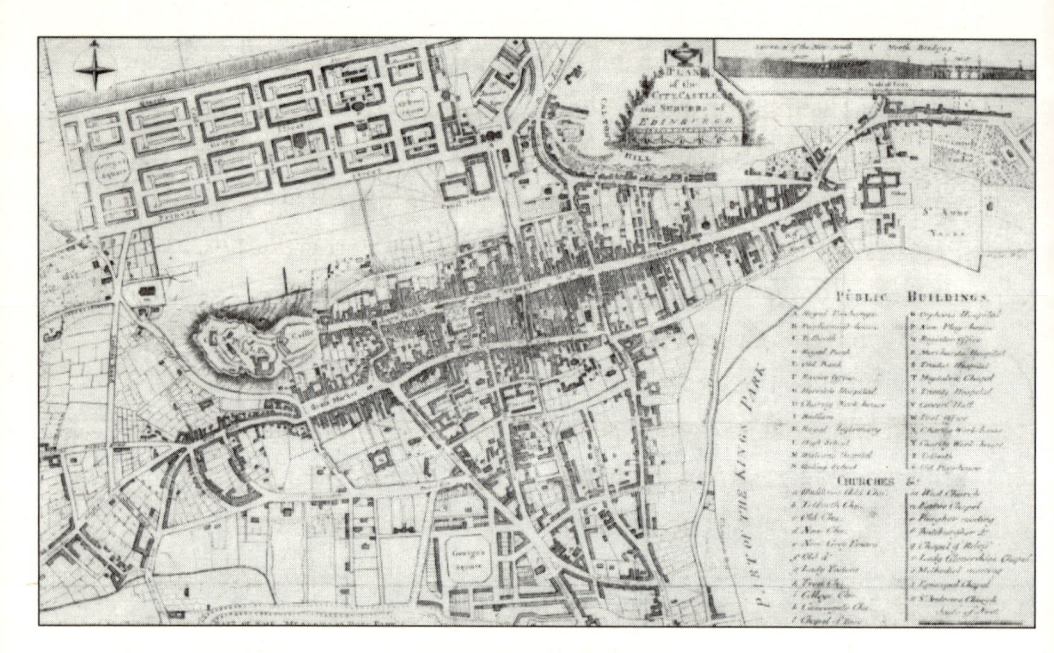

Edinburgh, in the middle of the eighteenth century, resembled a fishbone.
George's Square was built on the southern edge of the city.
Later, the New Town was built to the north.
(Reproduced with the permission of the National Library of Scotland)

The new Edinburgh – and what it represented – was obvious. The main streets of the New Town were named Queen Street, George Street and Princes Street: they placed King George in the middle, with the queen on one side and the princes on the other. In between these, there were Rose Street and Thistle Street: the emblems of Scotland and England in parallel. At either end of these streets were large squares, St Andrew's Square and St George's Square: the patron saints of Scotland and England in symmetry. That, at least, was the original plan, though by the time that St George's Square was built, it had been renamed (to avoid confusion with George Square).[7]

After the New Town was built, and as it expanded over the decades, Edinburgh began to look very different. What was once an overcrowded, unsanitary and often unruly city – it was said that 'walking the streets of Edinburgh at night was pretty perilous and a good deal odoriferous' – became a grand city: the 'Athens of the North'.[8] It was the modern capital of 'North Britain'. 'Edinburgh' now referred to a very different place.

When we look at things out there in the world – at Edinburgh, or George Square, or the former David Hume Tower – we don't see them as they really are. Whatever we notice, we see it as *something*. We give it a name. And that name matters. It tells us what we're looking at. It allows us to describe it to others. It allows others to describe it to us. However, for that to work properly, we need to know what the name means. What, precisely, are we talking about?

This isn't obvious. Names change over time. The meaning of names can vary. So, they can be interpreted in different ways. The David Hume Tower was a building named after a great philosopher. Or a building named after a racist. 'Edinburgh' is a name, but what does it mean? It used to describe a smaller place. Today, it describes a bigger place. Even today, it depends on who's talking. To a student, 'Edinburgh' means the university: it's the institution that they attend. To a stand-up comedian, 'Edinburgh' means the Fringe: it's a run of gigs that they do. To a Westminster politician, 'Edinburgh' is the parliament and, to a tourist, 'Edinburgh' is a destination. To a Glaswegian, 'Edinburgh' is that place full of [insert the appropriate name here]'. To me [one of them], 'Edinburgh' is home. Depending on who's talking about 'Edinburgh', they might be describing very different things.

This isn't merely a local matter. We hear people talk about 'Scotland' and 'Britain', 'Europe' and 'America'. In the process, they talk about 'independence', 'democracy', 'greatness' and 'freedom'. However, it's not obvious what they mean. These generally sound like good things (which is why these names are used), though they might refer to very different things (which, of course, they do). The names that we use can have different meanings.

Names, and what they represent to us, are fundamental to whatever we think. As the artist Simon Munnery has pointed out, there must be things that we haven't named, but it's very difficult to think of any.[9] The names that we use, and the meanings that they have, define every single thing that we think about.

We interpret what we notice, and what we're told by others, through words that have particular meanings. It's part of the window through which we view the world in which we live. However, there are always different perspectives. So, when someone else describes something, we need to know what *they* mean.

To see the bigger picture, we need to consider alternative perspectives. To do this, I'm going to wander up to Bristo Square, just a couple of minutes away.

I'm on Bristo Square, looking at a map of the local area. It shows the location of the university buildings. Near the bottom of the map, there's a text box that tells you (in confident bold letters): **You Are Here**.

I'm reading it now. Therefore, it's true.

Sometimes, when you read something, it just seems obvious. The things that we read can be very convincing. For example, right now, you are here, reading *this*. And now, at this moment, you are here, reading *this*. But these statements are only true from a specific point of view. From *here*, for example, neither is true. So, we need to consider different points of view.

How we interpret things

There are several maps on Bristo Square, located in different positions. Each map shows a slightly different view of the local area. However, each one tells you the same thing: You Are Here. Each one of them, when you read it, is convincing.

So, I'm now stepping back to get a wider perspective. From the edge of Bristo Square, I have a view of all these maps. I can see their different positions. And I can see why, from this or that position, each one seems convincing. I can now see the bigger picture.

Everything that we read – every description of something – every claim that this or that is the case – is written from a certain position. What it means depends on the context. In this case, the claim that 'You Are Here' simply means that – in the context of you being able to read *this* map, and in relation to the buildings represented on *this* map – this is your current position. If you understand the context, then you know what it means. As a result, you know where you are. To get a sense of perspective, you need to consider the position from which a claim is made.

However, depending on the context, it will present a particular view of things. It will offer you a *particular* picture. For example, the maps around here show the location of the nearby university buildings. However, they don't include the nearby shops and cafés, or the trees and paths in the gardens. They show the buildings as flat shapes. They don't show what the buildings really look like. They make some things obvious. They exclude other things. They show you only what's thought to be relevant.

This is because a map is a description. Like all descriptions, it describes the real world – *but only some of it*. A map represents the real world by including some things and leaving out others. It shows what the cartographer thinks is relevant. And this is what all descriptions do: they describe what the describer thinks is relevant. They present a particular view, which directs your attention to this not that.

For example, 'You Are Here' describes your location. It directs your attention to *this* thought, not something else, because *this* has been made relevant. 'You Are Here' makes you think about where you are. Not what you're doing: You're reading this. You're also breathing. However, you've not thought about that until now – because it's been brought to your attention. All of these claims are true. It's not simply a matter of truth. It's a matter of what's made relevant.

As we try to make sense of the world around us, we rely on the descriptions of others. Each one presents a particular picture: it makes *something* relevant and describes it in a *particular* way. Before we can consider the truth of the matter – before we can decide to accept or reject it – we've been led to think about *that* thing and to see it in *that* particular way. From the outset, descriptions shape how we think.

However, if we take the time to compare different descriptions, then we can see their limits. To do that, I'm going to head back to George Square ... but to a different location.

I'm now in the university library, on the south side of the square.

I came here to look at two maps of Edinburgh. One is an old map (c. 1750). It shows the Castle and the Palace, the High Street that connects them, and the dozens of narrow backstreets that once descended into darker places. The other is a present-day map of the same area. But this isn't a map of 'Edinburgh'. It's a map of the 'Old Town' of Edinburgh. The same area now has a different name.

How we interpret things

If you compare the two maps, then you can spot the differences. The old map includes buildings and streets that, since 1750, have been demolished. The present-day map of Edinburgh Old Town includes things that, since 1750, have been built (for example, George Square and the Scottish Parliament). By comparing it with the older map, you can see the changes with your own eyes.

But only some of them. For example, the Castle and the Palace have become huge tourist attractions, with guides and gift shops full of tacky souvenirs. The High Street is now a mile-long mall of cafés, pubs, and shops that sell anything tartan, anything that's made of wool, and anything else that's supposedly Scottish. Such things don't appear on this map because they're not considered relevant. In the real High Street, however, they matter. If you walk that road, then you'll see this with your own eyes.

If we compare the present-day map with the present *reality*, then we can see what's *really* missing. For example, the map shows George Square from a certain perspective. It's flat: a small green square surrounded by smaller rectangles. However, when I look out of the window of the library, I can see the *real* George Square: it has trees and railings and cobbles and windows and doors and people going from here to there. I can compare the George Square on the map with the real George Square, and I can spot the differences. I can do that because the two are observable. I can see the differences between them – what's included and excluded – with my own eyes.

But here's the thing: not all descriptions are so easy to compare with reality. So, it's harder to spot the differences. When you read or hear the descriptions of others, and you don't have access to what they describe, you need to rely on the words that they use, which have particular meanings. If you don't know what *they* mean, then you won't know what they're talking about. Meanwhile, they'll describe a particular picture, which includes only what they think is relevant. They'll direct your attention to this or that, and make no reference to the other. They'll provide a window through which you can look, which displays a limited number of things and presents them in a particular way.

Beyond this, there's a bigger picture. Beyond the map, there's the territory. And, when you can't see the territory, you need to be more curious about how the map has been drawn. Why have they included this or that? What do they mean by 'this' or 'that'? And what about the other: what are we missing?

Whatever your view of the world, it's based on what you notice and how you interpret it. Whatever you think – about politics, religion or anything else – is based on what others have told you. Nobody is born with a particular view about immigration, taxation or the welfare state. Nobody is born with a particular view about this or that god, or, for that matter, about how They might want us to behave. Your world-view is based on the descriptions of others, which offer a particular picture.

However, there are a range of options. You can't always compare a map to reality, but you can always compare different maps. You can consider alternative perspectives. To do that, you need to be more curious about the maps that we draw of the world of people and things, and about how we draw them.

Whatever your view of the world might be, it's something that you've constructed. The world doesn't make sense of itself. We need to *make* sense of it. We do that by creating a map of the territory. We make distinctions between this and that. We draw particular boundaries.

How we interpret things

We interpret the world of people and things in terms of countless categories. We create categories by seeing some things as similar and by distinguishing these from other things. When we see similarities between things, we group them together and treat them as a single category: we *generalise* about x or y (e.g. tables or chairs, fiction or non-fiction). When we see differences between things, we tease them apart and treat them as separate categories: we *discriminate* between x and y (e.g. tables versus chairs, fiction versus non-fiction). It's an act of mental filing that creates order out of chaos.

Categorisation – by grouping things together or teasing them apart – is fundamental to how we think. It's essential, therefore, to being able to think critically. Indeed, some critical thinking tests include questions that test your ability to spot similarities and differences. Here's one that I've used myself: which of these is the odd one out – one, two, three, the?

Sometimes, the answer seems obvious.

Now, here's a quick joke. A teacher says to the class: 'Which is the odd one out: Andy, Billy, Charlie, chocolate?' A wee girl puts her hand up and says: 'Billy.' The teacher is disappointed and asks: 'Why do you think that the answer is Billy?' And the wee girl replies: 'I don't like Billy.'

The wee girl was right: which is the odd one out depends on the rules. We group together and tease apart according to particular rules. This is something that's not covered by the odd-one-out question. It's just meant to be obvious.

Now, which is the odd one out: one, two, three, the? The answer should no longer seem obvious. It might be any one of them. It depends on the particular rule that we use: for example, the first

Radical Thinking

letter (one), the last letter (two), the number of letters (three), or the 'obvious' one (the).

Here's the point: we see the world in terms of categories, and these are based on certain criteria: on noticing *particular* differences or similarities. And here's the problem: we can categorise people and things in countless ways because, no matter what we're talking about, we can always find differences and similarities.

After all, identical twins aren't really identical: they have different names and live different lives. Two peas in a pod aren't really identical: they vary slightly in size and shape, and one is always to the left of the other. And, no matter how different two people might seem, they always have similarities. Hitler and Gandhi lived at the same time, had global influence, had surnames of six letters, and were both vegetarians (though not 100 per cent). They were also, genetically speaking, 99.9 per cent the same (though not 100 per cent).

Think of *any* two things, from *any* category (or, for that matter, from any two categories) – people, places, abstract concepts, sounds, smells, hedge fund managers, animals, vegetables, minerals – and they'll have something in common.[10]

So, when we look at the world of people and things, we group them together and tease them apart by noticing *particular* similarities and differences. Some are obvious, even here in the library: size and shape (e.g. tables or chairs), substance and colour (e.g. wood or metal furniture), proximity (e.g. one study space or another). We do the same with people: by height and width, hair and clothes, near and far. We can see these differences with our own eyes.

However, we've also made many other forms of discrimination available. And these have become increasingly relevant: age, sex, class, occupation, race, ethnicity, nationality, religion, sexuality, sexual identity, etc. We've categorised each other in countless ways. We then see others as one of us, or as one of them, depending on the relevant criteria. And these criteria – the ones that we think are relevant – determine who is the odd one out.

We all fit into countless categories, but we tend to notice some, not others. We might distinguish between people on the basis of the colour of their eyes, on the basis of the colour of their hair, or on the basis of the colour of their skin. But we've tended to discriminate in particular ways. Some categories have been more obvious than others, not because they naturally matter, but because we've made them relevant.

This has real-world implications: it leads us to think in particular ways and it shapes how we interpret what we see and hear.

For example, we tend to notice the way that people look and speak, and then make certain assumptions about them. We draw on stereotypes, which we carry in our heads, to represent different kinds of people: the blonde, the inner-city youth, the single mother, the hard-working British people, the Muslim. I'm thinking of one individual who could be described in all of these ways. She was a student. The categories that we use, even if accurate, paint a particular picture.

When we read or hear from a person, the way that we categorise that person shapes how we interpret what they say. In the case of a claim about gender (or race), it makes a difference if it comes from a woman (or from a person of colour). In the case of a claim about health (or education), it matters if it comes from a doctor (or a teacher). Some categories of people are seen as more entitled than others to talk about certain topics.[11] As a result, they seem more convincing.

This is why, when politicians wish to convince us, they place themselves in a relevant category. When they speak about discrimination, they speak 'as a woman' or 'as a person of colour' (or, if they can't do that, then 'as a parent with daughters' or as 'as the son of immigrants'). After all, if you speak about discrimination 'as a white man', then it may sound less convincing.

We make sense of the world by interpreting everything that we see and hear through a filter. We carve up the world of people and things by distinguishing between this and that – according to *particular* criteria. In the process, we draw particular boundaries to create a map, which describes the world of people and things in a certain way. It's populated by a set of categories, to which we give names, which have certain meanings. These become the foundations of our knowledge: we learn the facts about *this* or *that*. It makes certain kinds of people more appealing than others. We're not surprised to learn *this* about *them*. We're less inclined to believe people like *that*.

What we notice, and how we interpret this or that, are constantly shaped by the categories that we think are obvious, that we have available, that we find appealing, or that we think are relevant. But we can all be categorised in countless ways. I'm a white man, which may be obvious, but I rarely make these two categories relevant because, while they're certainly available, if I were to do so, then it wouldn't be appealing. Meanwhile, I'm also a Scot, a Brit, a European, a citizen of the world, and a human being. I'm a brother, a partner, a voter, a taxpayer, who has been many things and am now other things. Like each of you, I'm many kinds of people and, when I say anything, I'm all these things.

But to my mother, I'm a son. To my students, I'm a teacher.

When they look at me, or hear what I say, it's through the frame of the particular category that seems obvious and relevant to them. And, of course, I do the same with others. No person is just one thing but, when we notice other people, we place them into one category or another, which represents only one thing about them. The maps that we draw of people and things represent one aspect of the territory. However, there are always other maps that can be drawn.

This is how we make sense of a world with an endless variety of things and people. We draw particular boundaries, which create the categories that we take for granted. These shape how we interpret what we see and hear. We can't avoid discrimination itself because it's fundamental to how we think. Even when we try to be less discriminatory, we need to discriminate between bigotry and tolerance, inequality and equality, and so on.

However, we can think about the bigger picture: the ways that people make distinctions and the reasons that they do. Both racists and anti-racists have made race relevant. Both sexists and feminists have made gender relevant. However, they've done it in different ways. Anti-racists and feminists have reacted to forms of discrimination that were already relevant, and which have had significant real-world effects that were obvious to them, but less obvious to others. In the process, these distinctions have become more visible, but the *meanings* of these distinctions have changed.

The distinctions that we draw are everywhere. We tend to take them for granted – not just the distinctions but what they mean – as if they're natural. However, the bigger picture is only visible when we see and hear alternative perspectives. We don't *need* to agree with them. We need only accept what they make obvious:

Radical Thinking

that an unfamiliar view reminds us that we have a view, and that it's limited.

They remind us that there are other ways of seeing things.

There are always other ways to organise our thoughts. Some ways may be better than others, but the only way to know is to consider the options.

For example, here in the university library, a few years ago, they changed the shelving system from the Dewey Decimal Classification to the Library of Congress Classification. The Dewey Decimal scheme divided books into ten categories: General Works; Philosophy; Religion; Social Sciences; Language; Pure Science; Technology; Arts; Literature; and History. Psychology books were in the Philosophy section. If a psychologist had visited the library, then they would have been told that their subject was part of philosophy. That would have annoyed them. However, for that to happen, a psychologist would have had to visit the library.

The Library of Congress scheme has twice as many sections (for example, there are sections on Law, Medicine and Political Science, and there are three sections on History). It also combines a few of the old ones (such as Language and Literature). Psychology is now part of a combined section: Philosophy, Psychology and Religion. If a psychologist were to visit the library now, then they'd be told that they were in the same section as philosophy and religion. That would make them furious. No wonder they never go to the library.

At first, the new system was a mild inconvenience. It took a little longer to find what I was after. This was, in part, because the library continued to use the Dewey system for older books. As a historian of psychology, I had to consult both new books, which were classified in one way, and old books, which were classified in a different way. However, now that I had to do this, I noticed both and spotted the differences.

I noticed that books that had long been neighbours now found themselves on separate floors. Meanwhile, books that had once been far apart were now having to mingle. They stared across the aisle at strangers, wondering what they had in common. A book on experimental psychology and a book on miracles now found themselves uncomfortably close. Like a member of the royal family trying to make small talk with a member of the public. Conversations with strangers who come from different positions can be difficult.

Now that the books had been grouped together and teased apart according to new rules, this had implications for how they were seen. Philosophy, Psychology and Religion was Class B, with Psychology being a subclass: BF. This included phrenology, palmistry and parapsychology, not to mention the occult (such as ghosts, witchcraft and astrology). If a psychologist had visited the library, then they might have complained: why had they been lumped together with pseudoscience, such as astrology, when they had nothing in common? Nevertheless, someone else clearly thought that they belonged in the same category.

That said, it could have been worse: books on the Bible were classified as BS.

One of the practical implications of the change in classification was that, as I looked at the shelves, I noticed books that I'd not seen before. Previously, I'd not considered them relevant to my own area of interest. However, now I took a closer look and made connections that, under the previous system, I wouldn't have made. I was diverted from my narrow search by other books, with other perspectives, which hadn't previously been on my radar.

And it began to feel like a metaphor for how we think about the world:

I visit the library less often now. The real world is so messy and unpredictable. I search online and quickly find what I'm looking for. It's easy and efficient because it narrows the focus. However, it limits my view to what I can see through the window that's already in my head.

Like everyone else, I have my own books. I picked them up along the way. At the time, they were obvious books to get or, perhaps, they were easily available. I found them appealing or thought they were relevant. They're grouped into a handful of loose categories that make sense to me. There are far too few books, and they cover too few topics, for a larger scheme to be needed. I buy new books, but not that many. After all, there's limited shelf space.

I suppose I could throw out some of the older books, but it's hard to discard what feels familiar. They'll likely sit there in the background, always available, as a quietly reassuring but remarkably limited collection of ideas.

But what else to do?

Well, I could categorise my books in a different way. If I tried a larger system, such as the Dewey or Library of Congress scheme, then I'd notice how much I was missing. The gaps in my collection would be obvious. I'd be more aware of the limits of what I read, and of how I've categorised things in old and familiar ways.

I'd probably feel the need to buy more books to fill the obvious gaps and, if necessary, discard some old ones. Or perhaps even invest

How we interpret things

in a few more shelves. Then I'd need to rearrange my collection so that the order made more sense.

My bookshelves would look different now. The old books would be surpassed and surrounded by newer and other books. 'My book collection' would now refer to something else. It would still be a fraction of what's out there, but it would be a larger fraction, and it would be a less random selection.

I wonder what this new arrangement might look like, and how it might differ from my current set? I can imagine that it would be like looking at a newer and larger map, which represented more of what's out there, and did so in different ways. A map with boundaries too freshly drawn to pretend that they've always been there.

But I'd need to look for unfamiliar content. I'd need to be prepared to revise my system. If I did that, then I'd be looking at a bigger picture.

* * *

Meanwhile, you are here.

You're reading this. You're thinking about this, not something else, because this is being brought to your notice. You're currently missing what else is going on: the outside world, the paragraphs above, and the number of words in this sentence.

As you're looking at this, you're interpreting it. You're not seeing what's really here. You're *making* sense of these squiggles on the page. You're transforming them into words and sentences which have particular meanings. You're drawing *particular* boundaries: between words and sentences but not between individual letters.

Radical Thinking

Words and sentences are the categories, in this context, which are relevant.

However, people see things differently. An infant sees the squiggles but not words and sentences. A non-English speaker sees the words and the sentences but not the meaning. A proofreader sees errors that I don't notice, and you may notice the occasional error what I am make. You know what I mean, but you still notice the error. Errors depend on rules, and you notice when rules are. Broken. But the. Rules about words and sentences

and paragraphs.

Are ones that we've created. We might have arranged things differently. After all, in different times and cultures, others have arranged things differently. And, if we encounter an ancient and foreign language or. A sudden change in arrangements then. We're reminded of this.

The unfamiliar brings to our notice the conventions that we follow. But, here and now, where things seem so familiar – where we're playing by the same rules – we don't notice that there are rules. We look through the window and see what's there. We don't notice the window itself – the meaning of the words that we use to refer to things, the descriptions that make particular things relevant, the categories that we take for granted – which frames our view of it all.

To see past the view that the window provides, we need to look at things from different perspectives. From the window on the east side of the library, for example, I can see the Radical Road. It appears to divide Salisbury Crags in two. Above it, I can see the hard brown rock. Below it, I can see green gorse and grass. This creates a visual boundary, which seems obvious: I can see it with my own eyes. It's based on particular criteria: above versus below; brown versus green.

When you actually walk the Radical Road, however, you see things differently. What you see depends on your position. From the top of the road, everything is below you. From the bottom of the road, everything is above you. The distinction between brown and green is less obvious because there are many different colours. And, as you look to the left or to the right, you understand that, if you changed direction, then things would be the other way round. You can see that the distinctions that we make – on the basis of colour, or above versus below, or left versus right – aren't fixed.

When you walk the Radical Road, you can see things that I can see from here, but from a different point of view. From there, you can see the building formerly known as the David Hume Tower. However, from there, it just looks like a building, which might be called anything at all. From there, you can see the Old Town and the New Town, but the boundaries aren't obvious. You might draw different ones. You can also see the library on George Square but, from there, it's not obvious that it's a library. It might contain anything and it might arrange its contents in various ways.

From there, you get a different perspective. You can see that your view of the world depends on your current position and direction of travel. You can see that, beyond your current position, different names might be used, different boundaries might be drawn, and things might be arranged differently. At some level, we already know this but, to notice it, we normally need to travel farther. For example, when we travel to a foreign land, we notice that things have different names. We find that people are categorised differently, including us, because we're now the foreigners. We find that they arrange their

Radical Thinking

world – at home and at work, in education and health, in religion and politics – in different ways. If we spend enough time there, when we return we realise that how we do things here is merely one way of doing things. However, we shouldn't need to travel so far to appreciate that this is the case.

The Radical Road is currently closed, but the path to radical thinking is not. Your world-view is based on how you interpret what you see and hear. However, if you're curious, then you can look farther, beyond the obvious things and the obvious ways in which you interpret them.

To do this, you need to consider alternative views, and you need to question what you take for granted. However, to see a wider range of views, we'll need a bit of altitude. And, to notice what we take for granted, we'll need a bit of distance.

So, for the next two chapters, I'll need to shift from my current position.

4

Our points of view

I've walked from the university library to the south-east side of the square: to 40 George Square (the building formerly known as David Hume Tower). I did this because it's the tallest building in the area. I took the lift to the twelfth floor. From here, there are some extraordinary views.

A view of the Nelson Monument, from the twelfth floor of 40 George Square.

Radical Thinking

As I look north, I can see Calton Hill. At the top of the hill is the Nelson Monument. It was built to commemorate Nelson's victory, in 1805, at the Battle of Trafalgar. The monument, which stands 100 feet high, is in the shape of a telescope, which is pointing downwards. As I look at it now, I see a giant telescope that, despite its enormous size, can't see beyond its own foundations.

That's because, from here, I can see both the giant telescope *and* the foundations on which it stands. So, I can see why, as a telescope, its view is limited. The problem is simple: to see beyond its current view, it needs to consider a different stance. After all, no matter how hard you look, you can only see what's in front of you.

Whatever your point of view might be – whatever you believe about this or that – it's based on foundations: the things that you take for granted. They sit quietly beneath the surface, supporting your current stance. In the process, they guide your view. They can seem so obvious that you can't see beyond them – until you consider alternative views.

In the next chapter, we'll consider some of these foundations. However, for the moment, we're going to consider different points of view. And some of them will seem extraordinary.

At the foot of Calton Hill is Waterloo Place, named after the Battle of Waterloo and the site of the old Waterloo Hotel. Charles Dickens stayed there while he was writing *Great Expectations*. In 1866, the Davenport brothers stayed there. Today, they're not well known, but Dickens knew who they were. In 1866, everyone knew who they were. And, when the Davenport brothers conducted a séance at the Waterloo Hotel, this was news.

By now, their career was on the decline. However, they could still attract an audience. They remained worthy of notice because, depending on what you believed, they were either exhibitors of a profound truth or else propagators of a terrible hoax. Arthur Conan Doyle believed that they were among the most important ambassadors of the truth of immortality.[1] Houdini believed that they were escape artists.[2]

In 1866, when the Davenport brothers came to Edinburgh, *The Scotsman* newspaper believed that they'd 'now dropt [*sic*] their spiritualistic pretensions; they no longer profess to be "mediums", but simply come forward as clever tricksters'.[3] That, however, wasn't quite true. The Davenports were doing what they'd always done. They were leaving it up to the audience to decide. People were free to believe what they wanted.

William and Ira Davenport were a curious pair, who provoked very strong views, of very different kinds, and occasional violence. They're little known today because one side of the argument was a clear winner. At the time, however, they managed to represent the full range of options – from which people were free to choose – on the matter of extraordinary beliefs. They're currently relevant because, if you understand the nature of extraordinary beliefs, then the nature of ordinary beliefs is much easier to understand.

A belief can be understood as a position taken towards a claim. For example, if you believe that it's raining, then you're taking a position towards the claim: 'it's raining'. Many beliefs are implicit. For example, I believe that 'I'm writing this' and you believe that 'I've written this', but such beliefs may not cross our minds until they're made explicit.[4] To understand beliefs, however, we need to make them explicit.

This is why extraordinary beliefs are a useful guide to what we believe. If you're told that it's raining, then you might grab an umbrella or wear a different coat, but you're unlikely to consider the matter deeply. If you're in Edinburgh, then it's hardly an extraordinary event. However, if you're told that a miracle has happened, then you're going to want to know more. What actually happened? How do you know? Are you sure that it might not have been something else? When something sounds extraordinary, you tend to be more curious about what to believe.

The beliefs that matter in the real world generally lie somewhere between the obvious and the extraordinary. It's raining. It's surprisingly heavy. There will be a flood. It's due to melting ice caps. This is caused by global warming. This is the result of human actions. We need to change the way that we use energy, or things will become catastrophic. Or, perhaps, it's all a hoax. When something sounds extraordinary, you tend to be more curious about what to believe.

This is why the Davenport brothers are an ideal lesson in how we come to hold the views that we do.

In the case of the Davenports, these were the facts.

They performed on stage with a large 'spirit cabinet', rather like a wardrobe. Inside the spirit cabinet were a wooden bench and a number of musical instruments: typically a guitar, a bell, a fiddle, a tambourine and a brass horn. The brothers sat on the bench and had members of the audience tie their hands and feet to the bench. The doors of the cabinet were then closed. A few moments later, strange noises were heard. The guitar strummed, the bell rang, the fiddle played and the tambourine shook. The brass horn and 'spirit hands' appeared through a gap in the door. However, when the doors of the cabinet were opened, the brothers were still tied up. So, how could these things have happened? The Davenport brothers didn't explicitly claim that this was due to the spirits. They let the audience make up their own minds.

There was more to it, but that was the basic demonstration that made them household names. It might not seem so extraordinary now, and not everyone found it extraordinary then, but it provoked a great deal of controversy at the time, which was what made them household names. The controversy was not about the facts: what people saw and heard with their eyes and ears. It was about how they interpreted the facts. Some believed that 'it was due to the spirits'. Others took the opposite position: they did *not* believe that 'it was due to the spirits'.

The belief that it was due to the spirits involved rejecting alternatives. The most obvious alternative, of course, was that the brothers were responsible for what happened. However, the demonstration was designed to rule this out. That was why the brothers were tied up. The cabinet stood on trestles so that it was obvious that no help could come from below the stage. They allowed the cabinet and ropes to be examined. They often asked for a member of the audience – a sailor, a scout or anyone else who knew how to tie a good knot – to tie them up. They allowed the knots to be checked later to confirm that they were still in place. Sometimes the knots were sealed and later the seals were checked: they remained intact. Sometimes, after their hands had been tied behind their backs, salt was placed in their hands: later, the salt was still in their hands. All of this was done to rule out the possibility that the brothers had strummed the guitar, played the fiddle, shaken the tambourine, rung the bell and so on. If it wasn't them, then it must have been the spirits. To some people, this was obvious.

Sometimes, however, when the Davenports were tied up, nothing happened. No strumming, no fiddling, no shaking, no ringing. For those who did *not* believe in spirits, the implications were obvious: clearly, the ropes had been tied too well and the brothers couldn't escape from them. When the brothers failed to deliver, this could provoke some violent reactions from those who had paid to see something more curious than, well, two men being tied up in a wardrobe. In Liverpool, for example, the audience stormed the stage and smashed the spirit cabinet to pieces.[5]

However, when the brothers failed to deliver, believers saw it differently. They pointed out that the brothers might have failed on this occasion, but they had succeeded on many other occasions. Furthermore, the fact that they'd failed on this occasion wasn't their fault: it was the fault of the spirits. The brothers were merely mediums and weren't in control of the spirits. They could only ask for the spirits to help, but it was up to the spirits to turn up. That was the nature of the spirits.

The Davenports also had their phenomena duplicated by stage conjurors, who built their own 'spirit cabinets', had themselves tied up with ropes, and made similar noises. They didn't explain how it was done, but they assured the audience that it was a trick. For most people, this was further evidence that the Davenports were frauds.

However, believers saw it differently. They claimed that it wasn't the same thing. The Davenports had also demonstrated *their* phenomena in private rooms, where sharp observers watched with careful scrutiny from just a few feet away. They'd succeeded not only on the stage but also in 'test conditions'.[6] Some spiritualists, on the other hand, believed that the performances of conjurors *were* similar: they believed that these were *also* the work of spirits. Of course, the stage conjurors denied this, but it was 'well known' that mediums were often reluctant to admit their powers. According to these believers, duplications of the Davenport phenomena weren't evidence of fraud: it was evidence of the spirits.

The Davenports were also caught cheating on more than one occasion. Or so it seemed to many. However, whether or not they'd really cheated was a matter of debate. And, in many cases, what looked like fraud could be interpreted as evidence of the spirits. For example, in a private séance, one of the brothers was seen walking around the room when he was supposed to be tied up. Rather than see this as evidence that he'd escaped from the ropes, this was believed to be a 'spirit double'. In another private séance, a sceptical observer smeared some ink on a 'spirit hand': after the lights went up, Ira Davenport's hand was covered in ink. Spiritualists suggested that the ink had been transferred from the spirit hand to the medium's hand (by the spirits).[7]

Even when spiritualists *accepted* that the Davenports had been caught cheating, this could *still* be interpreted as evidence of the spirits. They pointed out that the brothers might have cheated on this occasion, but they'd not cheated on other occasions. It was, they felt, a fact of death that spirits didn't always turn up. Under pressure to produce the goods, it was 'lamentably common that genuine mediums will occasionally "help the spirits"'.[8] Cheating mediums, they claimed, were an understandable reaction to the unreliable nature of the spirits. And, of course, it might not have been the mediums themselves who were cheating: it might have been due to bad spirits, who 'made the boys do what they were unconscious of doing themselves'.[9]

Radical Thinking

In other words, no matter the facts, they could always be interpreted as evidence of the spirits. To anyone who doesn't believe in spirits, this might seem extraordinary. However, it's not. The same kinds of arguments have been made ever since to justify belief in paranormal and supernatural phenomena. When a psychic fails in controlled conditions, it's only failure on *this* occasion. When magicians duplicate the same phenomena, *that* is not the same thing. When an evangelical preacher is convicted of fraud, it's only fraud on *this* occasion. When countless prayers aren't answered, but one is answered, then *this* is a miracle. When countless people die, but a few survive, then God has miraculously saved *them*.

If you do believe in the supernatural, then this shouldn't seem extraordinary. However, for most people who believe in the supernatural, some of it will. Some religious people believe in psychic phenomena, but many don't. Some believe in the powers of evangelical preachers, and others don't. Some believe in the power of prayer to produce miraculous events, but others don't. There are Christians who don't believe in miracles, even those in the Bible. Millions who believe in God, even in the same God, believe very different things.

And so, the lesson of this sermon is this: to understand belief, we need to think about what, *precisely*, people believe. To do that, we need to understand things from *their* point of view. This isn't difficult. People give their reasons. And, if we listen to them, then their beliefs may not seem so extraordinary.

People believed in spiritualism for many reasons, but the belief itself was this: spirits communicate with us by doing certain things. Spiritualists believed that these things were caused by the spirits, not by something else. They didn't believe that everything was caused by the spirits. Just certain things. And, if only one of these things was genuinely the result of the spirits, then spiritualism was true. After all, if a single miracle happens, then miracles are possible. Spiritualists, therefore, only had to believe that one or more phenomena were genuine.[10]

From that perspective, everything else made sense. It didn't matter if, in a particular séance, nothing happened. The fact that nothing happened on that occasion didn't mean that it never happened. It didn't matter if conjurors could do similar things by trickery, or if mediums were caught cheating. As spiritualists pointed out on a regular basis, the existence of counterfeit money doesn't mean that there's no genuine money.[11] This was one reason why the debunkers of spiritualism failed to convince them. They were pointing out that mediums failed in certain conditions, that conjurors could duplicate the phenomena, and that mediums often cheated. However, spiritualists already knew this. They frequently admitted this themselves. But they rarely changed their beliefs because their beliefs were based on *other* phenomena: the ones that they were convinced were genuine.

As a result, spiritualists were generally less sceptical about the reality of other phenomena, the testimony of others, and the honesty of mediums. Nevertheless, from their point of view, that was relatively unimportant compared to the bigger picture: that when we die, we survive. That was an appealing belief and one worth hanging on to. In any case, what was the alternative?

The alternative, in this case, was rather popular. Most people didn't believe that the Davenport phenomena were the work of spirits. They might not have known how it was done, but they assumed that it was a trick, much like the tricks of stage conjurors. And most

Radical Thinking

people didn't believe in spiritualism at all. They'd read and heard about the many reports of extraordinary phenomena that had happened at séances. Or, rather, which witnesses *claimed* had happened. However, they believed that these witnesses were unreliable: they had inadequate eyes and ears.

This is sometimes described as 'disbelief'. However, it was a belief: that there were no genuine phenomena. This belief assumed that they all could be attributed to ordinary explanations (such as fraud, coincidence, misinterpretation, gullibility, wishful thinking, bias, etc.). 'Disbelievers' didn't *know* this. They didn't witness all the phenomena. Even the most ardent sceptics attended only a handful of séances. However, that didn't matter. Whatever other witnesses claimed, it could always be interpreted in terms of ordinary explanations (such as fraud, coincidence, misinterpretation, gullibility, wishful thinking, bias, etc.). Any reported miracle can be explained in these ways. They cover any impossibility. In other words, no matter the facts, they could always be interpreted in line with 'disbelief', i.e. the belief that such things do *not* happen.

The Davenports, and their extraordinary phenomena, reveal something remarkably ordinary. For the last two centuries, at least, this has been the debate about paranormal and supernatural phenomena. On the one side are the believers: they believe that extraordinary things can happen because, in one or more cases, there seems to be no ordinary explanation. On the other side are the 'disbelievers': they believe that there's always an ordinary explanation, even if they don't know what it is. All the facts can be, and have been, interpreted in line with either of these beliefs.

That's why the debate will continue.

Our beliefs about ordinary things are similar.

They involve rejecting alternatives.[12] For every belief, there's at least one alternative. You can believe that it's raining (or that it's not). You can believe that the ice caps are melting (or not). If you see them with your own eyes, of course, then you're likely to accept the facts. However, you can interpret the facts in different ways. You can believe that the ice caps are melting due to a natural fluctuation in temperature (or that it's due to global warming). You can believe that global warming is due to human actions (or that it's not). You can believe that climate change will become catastrophic (or that it won't).

Even when the facts appear to contradict your beliefs, they can be interpreted so that they support your beliefs. After all, we continue to believe in things even when they fail to happen. We try again. We live in hope. We might call this wishful thinking. Or perseverance. We continue to believe, even when the facts can be explained in a different way. We prefer our *own* interpretation of events. We might call this bias. Or conviction. We continue to believe, even when we discover that there are cases of fraud. We might call this gullibility. Or pragmatism. After all, there are frauds in every walk of life.

Sometimes, however, people seem to do this to an extraordinary degree. When a political leader fails to deliver what he promised, believers continue to believe. It wasn't his fault. It was the fault of unseen powers: the deep state that controls us all. If he denounces the actions of others, then does the same thing, believers continue to believe. It's *not* the same thing. And, even if it *is* the same thing, it was justified (on this occasion). When he's exposed, as a liar or a cheat, believers continue to believe. They don't believe the facts: they're fake news, the propaganda of unseen powers. Whatever the facts – the *reported* facts – they're interpreted as evidence of invisible powers.

The conventional way to think about such beliefs – the ones that *we* find extraordinary – is to ask ourselves: why do *they* think *that*? We can then come up with some reasons why others get things wrong. We can explain their beliefs in terms of misinterpretation, gullibility, wishful thinking, bias, etc. There's a large psychological literature on the question of why we get things wrong. This has been called the 'psychology of error', which psychologists use to explain why people hold erroneous beliefs.[13] In the nineteenth century, when the discipline of Psychology began, psychologists used it to explain why people believed in spiritualism. Since then, it's been used to explain all kinds of beliefs that psychologists regard as wrong. They can all be explained in terms of misinterpretation, gullibility, wishful thinking, bias, etc.

This may be true, but it's not the whole truth. After all, we're all prone to misinterpretation, gullibility, wishful thinking, bias, etc. And, if we get things wrong, then these might be the reasons why. But how do we know if we got it wrong? The 'psychology of error' may explain *why* we get things wrong, but it doesn't tell us *which* things are wrong. In psychological experiments, we know what's true because the experimenter is in control of the conditions: the rules are fixed and the facts are known. In the real world, however, this is rarely, if ever, the case. We assume that certain beliefs are wrong, then explain why errors are made. In the real world, if we explain the beliefs of others as the result of error, then we're assuming that *they* have made an error. We're assuming that *we* have got it right.

If we wish to understand beliefs, then a more radical way is needed. No belief is certain: it depends on the interpretation of limited facts. And, whatever you believe, it will depend not only on the facts but also on the context. After all, what you find *extra*-ordinary (or *para*-normal, or *super*-natural) depends on what you think is ordinary (or normal, or natural). And that's a matter of context.

What now seems ordinary, normal or natural isn't the same as it used to be. In 1866, when the Davenports came to town, women (and nine out of ten men) had no vote, acts of 'sodomy' were liable to a minimum of ten years' imprisonment, and the age of consent was twelve. We can only wonder, had we lived then, what we would have believed was normal.

Meanwhile, what was once considered extraordinary, so far as it was considered at all, is now taken for granted. As we walk down the street, talking to someone in another part of the world, using a small device that can also play music, has access to endless information – including how many steps that we've taken – we think that *this* is normal. In 1866, if you'd thought this, then you'd have been considered a lot stranger than a spiritualist.

What we believe largely depends on the context in which we live. If you live in a context in which belief in miracles is taken for granted, then you're unlikely to question it. In 1866, belief in miracles was the norm. However, belief in spiritualism was *not* the norm. Most people believed in the miracles of the Bible but not in the phenomena of spiritualism. Yet, as many pointed out, the evidence for spiritualism was better.[14] It wasn't just a matter of facts.

Whatever we believe, it's not just about the facts. It depends on what we take for granted: the (seemingly) ordinary, normal and natural. It also depends on the options, here and now, that are available. Whatever our individual beliefs might be – about politics, religion or anything else – they don't begin inside our heads. They're always part of a bigger picture, which provides us with some options.

People make observations and interpret them. They then claim that this or that is the case. Others then respond to these claims by taking a particular position towards them: some believe this and some believe that. People then argue about this and that. In the process, they create a menu of beliefs from which you're free to choose. Whatever you choose, however, it's limited to what's available on the menu. And, over time, as new things happen, claims are made and positions are taken, the menu changes.

When you make your choice, of course, you want to base *your* belief on the facts. However, each of the options on the menu is presented in a way that seems plausible. Every option involves a claim: that this or that is the case. For example, the spirits are real, or God exists, or the government can't be trusted. Every claim is linked to a description: that this or that has happened. For example, a medium knew the name of my childhood pet, or we prayed to God and my sister got better, or the government told us that they'd cut taxes, but then they raised them. These descriptions are presented as facts. But, even if the facts are true, as we discussed in the last chapter, descriptions paint a particular picture. They describe the facts, but only some of them – they include some things and leave out others – and present them in a particular way. If only one side of the argument is available to you – whether it's about politics, religion or anything else – then you'll likely be convinced.

That's why you need to consider different perspectives: to understand what the options are. You can then make a more informed choice, based on a larger menu of options, from which you're free to choose.

But, having done that, how do you choose which one to believe? This will depend on your current position. The more extraordinary something seems to you, the harder it will be for you to believe. But if you're willing to change your mind, what would it take for you to do so? Since you see only a fraction of what's out there, you need to rely on the word of others. But whom to trust? In the real world, this has increasingly become the problem. Everyone has a view, which they constantly describe, and all of them do their best to sound convincing.

If you wish to base your beliefs on the facts, then you can't rely on an individual view. You need to rely on all the available evidence. On any given topic, there are communities of experts who spend their careers examining all the available evidence. They may argue about how to interpret the facts. They often disagree. They don't offer certainty. But they know considerably more than we do. That, of course, is what makes them experts.

This is why, when non-experts challenge experts, they're often 'just asking questions'. But the questions that they ask make *something* relevant. For example, how many vaccinated people get sick? They direct your attention to that not this: how many unvaccinated people get sick? Experts have already asked these questions, and many others. They may disagree on the answers and, even if they do, these answers don't offer certainty. That's why an individual view, even that of an expert, isn't enough. The combined knowledge of the relevant community of experts is the best that we have. However, you're always free to believe otherwise, if you think that you know better.

I'm an expert on certain things. For example, I've studied the history and psychology of magic and the paranormal for twenty-five

Radical Thinking

years. I've seen nothing (with my own eyes) to convince me that paranormal phenomena exist. We see only a fraction of what's going on, of course, so I might be missing something. I've looked farther. I've spoken to others and I've read countless eyewitness reports. But there are many frauds, and I know enough about deception to know that anyone can be deceived. So, when someone assures me that they weren't deceived, I'm not convinced. There are strange coincidences, but I know enough about probability to know that, in a world of countless events, strange coincidences are inevitable. There are, I think, a few cases that are more mysterious than the debunkers would have you believe. And, if only one of them is real, then such things are possible.

But whatever the facts, they must be interpreted. There are the things that people have seen (with their own eyes) and there are the ways in which they've been interpreted. They've been interpreted as explicable (according to the laws of science), i.e. as the result of fraud, coincidence, etc. They've been interpreted as inexplicable (according to the laws of science), i.e. as evidence of paranormal or supernatural forces. I've studied the rhetoric of debunkers and proponents, who all appeal to the facts – but only some of them – and describe them in a particular way, as each side accuses the other of misinterpretation, bias, etc. If you only hear one side of the argument, and if it fits with your current position, then this will simply be reinforced.

However, if you read the best arguments of those with whom you disagree, then you'll see the bigger picture. You don't need to believe them. I began as a sceptic and I remain one (though, as a sceptic, I know that I might be wrong). I'm not neutral. None of us is neutral. All of our beliefs are based on limited facts. However, my reason for not being converted is that I think the facts are *too* limited. If paranormal phenomena were real, then I'd expect the evidence to be significantly better. Until that happens, I remain a sceptic. You're free, of course, to believe what you want.

Meanwhile, I have beliefs about many things on which I've no expertise. For example, for the last fifty years, scientists have warned about the effects of human actions on climate change. It began with a handful of experts, though most experts were initially sceptical. Over the following decades, the evidence grew and scientists increasingly changed their minds. Meanwhile, in the real world, the debate continued. The facts were interpreted in different ways: they were attributed to fraud, coincidence, misinterpretation, wishful thinking, bias, etc. Today, however, there's a consensus among scientists (of over 99 per cent). Nevertheless, the debate continues because some people think they know better.

I'm no expert on this. I don't know better. So, on this topic, I believe the experts. That's why I believe that the ice caps are melting, that this is caused by global warming, and that this is the result of human actions. I believe that we need to change the way that we use energy, or else things will become catastrophic.

And, right now, I believe that it's raining.

As we choose from the available menu of beliefs, we need to remember that the menu is limited. We need to consider what we're missing. There are more options than we think and, without adequate options, there's little choice. There is, of course, the illusion of choice. We're free to choose from the beliefs that are available to us, but the same two political parties always win and, if the winning candidate isn't a Christian, then their victory was in spite of that. We're free to choose from countless brands, which are owned by a handful of companies and barely distinguishable from each other. We're free to choose from countless sports shoes, but pity the youngster who decides to wear sandals.

In other ways, however, the menu is growing. In a virtual world, in which all voices can be heard, beliefs that once would have remained in the shadows are now seeing the light of day. And they're finding an audience of sceptical folk who are sceptical about what *we* take for granted: that the earth is round, that facts are facts, that experts know more than we do. We're surrounded by conspiracy theories, alternative facts and other extraordinary views. As we'll see later, if you're curious, then you can make sense of them all.

However, to do that, you can't just dismiss them. You need to remember that all of us – whatever our views might be – notice only limited facts, which we then interpret. And, as we've seen, whatever the facts, you can always interpret them in a way that supports your *own* beliefs. To avoid this, you need to consider the views of others: *from their point of view*. This provides a sense of perspective. You don't need to agree with them. You need only accept what they make obvious: that all beliefs are based on interpreting limited facts and, therefore, you might be wrong.

Whatever your beliefs, they have their limits. They've been selected from the available options. Your choices have been shaped by what you think is ordinary, normal or natural. In other words, they're based on certain assumptions: the things that you take for granted. These can seem so obvious that you don't question them. It's not easy to see past the foundations that support your current stance. Even a giant telescope, pointing downwards, sees no farther. Unlike the views of others, though, the things that you take for granted are inside your head. You can't see them with your own eyes. The most powerful telescope in the world can't view the space between its lenses.

You can, however, think about them. If you think in a radical way, you can examine the foundations that support your current stance. But you need to do this at ground level. So, it's time for a wee walk.

5

Local customs and habits

For the moment, the rain has stopped. So, let's go on a brief tour. It's time to look at some of the things we take for granted. As we'll see, the assumptions we make are shaped by the customs and habits of the time and place in which we live.

I'm leaving George Square and going round the corner. I'm crossing Bristo Square, where several different maps are telling me that I'm here. I'm now passing the statue of Greyfriars Bobby, the wee terrier famous for sitting for fourteen years by his master's grave. His loyalty earned him this statue, a bad Walt Disney film, and the attention of millions of tourist cameras. Just past Bobby, on George IV Bridge, is the Elephant House, the café that J. K. Rowling visited when she was writing her early books. A large sign now sits in the café window: 'the birthplace of Harry Potter'. Tourists now pay more attention to this café than to poor old Bobby. So much for loyalty. I'm now arriving at the High Street, where I can see, with my own eyes, the statue of David Hume.

As I get closer, I can see his right toe shimmering in the timid Edinburgh sun. This is the result of a local custom. Shortly after the statue appeared, a rumour also appeared: that rubbing Hume's toe would bring good luck. Since then, countless passers-by have rubbed his toe and made it shiny. They've turned the great sceptic, the enemy of superstition, into a talisman of magical thinking.[1]

Hume was known for being a sceptic. In one of his famous arguments, he doubted the most extraordinary things. Imagine being told that a miracle has happened. For example, someone claims that they witnessed (with their own eyes) a resurrection. That's evidence, but we need to weigh up the evidence. After all, we know that testimony can be unreliable. People sometimes lie and they often misremember things. Against this claim, there's the combined experience of everyone else. That's why a resurrection is a miracle: it contradicts our common experience that, when people die, they remain dead. When we compare the alternatives and weigh up the evidence, which is more likely: that the testimony is wrong or that someone rose from the dead? Hume thought it was bound to be the former.

Hume's argument continues to be used by sceptics of the paranormal. They point out that extraordinary claims contradict our common experience. So, in the words of Carl Sagan: 'extraordinary claims require extraordinary evidence.'[2] If you tell me that you saw an aeroplane flying, then I'll take you at your word. If you tell me that you saw an elephant flying, then I'm going to need more than that. Mind you, if I'd never seen or heard of such a thing as an aeroplane, then I'd have good reason to be sceptical about that. According to Hume, that would be a sensible position, because it contradicts my experience. And, since he'd never seen an aeroplane, he'd have been sceptical too.

Our knowledge is based on experience, but our experience is always limited. So, we assume that things beyond our experience

Radical Thinking

resemble things that we've seen. This was another of Hume's famous arguments. He also doubted the most obvious things: things that we take for granted. We assume, for example, that the sun will rise tomorrow because, in our experience, the sun has risen every day. So, we expect this to happen in the future. But tomorrow is another day. Therefore, we can't be certain what will happen. That said, Hume expected the sun to rise. His point was that this is an expectation based on experience. It's a habit. But it doesn't follow that our experience in the future will be the same. In that sense, anything is possible.

Nothing is certain and anything is possible. So, what are you supposed to believe? Hume would say that you can rely on your experience, even if it's limited. If you've never seen or heard of an aeroplane, then you're quite right to be sceptical. However, that doesn't mean that you're correct. You might just want to get out more and widen your experience. If you haven't seen a miracle, then you're quite right to be sceptical. So, you might want to go out and see one. However, the fact that anything is possible doesn't mean that everything will happen. We've learned from collective experience that some things are significantly more likely than others.

Hume doubted all miracles when precious few did. He doubted whether the sun would rise tomorrow. However, even the great sceptic had his limits. When it came to matters of race, he took for granted what was a common view in that time and place. When he voiced his suspicion that 'other species of men' were 'naturally inferior to the whites', he justified this by saying that 'there never was a civilised nation of any other complexion than white, nor even any individual eminent either in action or speculation.'[3] He was unaware of this because his experience was limited. He thought that things beyond his experience resembled what he'd seen. When he heard of an exception to his view, 'a man of parts and learning', he assumed that this man was 'admired for slender accomplishments, like a parrot, who speaks a few words plainly'.[4] He regarded the very idea as extraordinary and required extraordinary evidence. His beliefs on this remained the same, the product of custom and habit.

But his views weren't entirely consistent. He did remain a sceptic about religion. In 1776, as he lay on his deathbed, he told James Boswell, the biographer of Samuel Johnson, that he found the idea of life after death a 'most unreasonable fancy'.[5] On some matters, however, he expressed different views. In other writings, he argued against not only slavery but also more general forms of discrimination. Experts disagree over what to make of this, but we can make some distinctions ourselves.

We can choose to disagree with his views on race and agree with what he said about other things. We needn't be loyal to everything that he said. We can embrace his ideas – but only some of them. And some of them are worth keeping in mind.

One of them is this: at the end of the day – and as sure as the sun will rise tomorrow – our beliefs will be short of certainty.

Since our experience is always limited, we need to make assumptions about the bigger picture. In different times and places, we make different assumptions. These, in turn, shape our thoughts. Here and now, I can see reminders of how our assumptions shape our thoughts about others.

For example, across the High Street from the David Hume statue is a cobbled mosaic: the Heart of Midlothian. It's local custom to

Radical Thinking

spit on it. Some believe that it brings good luck, but the custom began as an act of protest. It's the site of the Old Tolbooth, where locals were once imprisoned, tortured and hanged. In 1696, one of its residents was Thomas Aikenhead, a student at the University. He'd described the Old Testament as 'fables' and the miracles of Jesus as 'pranks'. He was arrested, imprisoned and charged with blasphemy. He was twenty years old, a first-time offender and, on Christmas Eve, he was sentenced to death. The Church of Scotland, when later asked if they wished to pardon the boy, declined. According to the Moderator of the Church of Scotland: 'the vigorous execution' of 'good laws' was needed to suppress 'impiety and profanity'.[6] Two days later, doubting Thomas was hanged. For expressing offensive beliefs.

The Old Tolbooth, where Thomas Aikenhead was imprisoned until he was hanged for expressing beliefs that others found offensive.

Just beyond the Heart of Midlothian is Parliament Square, the home of the highest court in the land: the Court of Session. In 1778, it considered the case of Joseph Knight. Knight had been bought as a slave in Jamaica, then brought to Scotland as a servant. Later, when he tried to leave his position, his master had him arrested. A lengthy legal battle then followed that ended up in the Court of Session. Knight was supported by Church of Scotland ministers. He was defended by Henry Dundas, who later became the most powerful politician in Scotland. He was supported by Boswell, who wrote to Johnson in praise of Dundas' contribution to the cause. The ruling of the Court was that 'the law of Jamaica, being unjust, could not be supported in this country'. It was, in effect, the abolition of slavery in Scotland.

Dundas went on to play a significant role in the abolition of the slave trade. However, at times he was against abolition.[7] Meanwhile, slavery continued in Jamaica, where Scots owned about 30 per cent of the plantations.[8] Later, when a third of the ministers of the Church of Scotland decided to form a new church – the Free Church of Scotland – they accepted money from slave-owners.[9] And Boswell later changed his mind: he wrote a poem that opposed abolition.[10] And Johnson, though he remained an opponent of slavery, had a black manservant who had been born into slavery on a Jamaican plantation. He also said some things about the Scots that many folk here found offensive.

David Hume. Henry Dundas. Church of Scotland ministers. Boswell and Johnson. They all did some good things and some bad things, according to what we now believe. And, depending on what we make relevant, we can either praise or condemn them. Just up the High Street is Edinburgh Castle. The entrance is guarded by statues of Robert the Bruce and William Wallace. These are our national heroes. In England, of course, they were seen as enemies. And, at various times, they were also the enemies of many Scots.

We all have our heroes and villains. It's one of our habits. When we rate people highly on one thing, we tend to rate them highly on other things. This is known as the 'halo effect'.[11] We tend to see people as saints or sinners. And, as we generalise about others, we attribute their actions to their disposition, rather than to the situation. This is such a common tendency that it's known as the 'fundamental attribution error'.[12] We see others as saints or sinners, and we ignore the context in which they do good or bad things.

If we wish to avoid fundamental errors, we need to think in a more radical way. Goodies and baddies are the stuff of children's stories. In the real world, people are limited and inconsistent. Depending on the time and place, and which of their actions we choose to make relevant, they can represent the good or the bad. This is one of the problems with statues: they're of individuals, rather than of values. The values that we wish to represent will vary, depending on time and place, and on what seems relevant to whom. These aren't set in stone. We can disagree, and change our minds, about what we think is good or bad.

We could, however, do something radical: we could agree to argue about 'good' versus 'bad', rather than about 'goodies' versus 'baddies'.

As I look farther up and down the High Street, I can see reminders of how our assumptions shape our thoughts about who we are.

I can see countless tourist shops on the street. In one of them, I bought a souvenir tea towel. It has a brief article printed on it, which lists a host of Scottish inventions and boasts of the inventiveness of the Scots. And, as is custom and habit here, it has a wee go at the English.

'Nowhere,' the tea towel declares in bold black print, 'can an Englishman turn to escape the ingenuity of the Scots.' At home, we're told by the tea towel, the Englishman depends on Scottish inventions, whether he's watching television or talking on the telephone. He could leave the house and get on his bike, but that was invented by a Scot. He could get in his car, but the tyres on which it runs were invented by John Dunlop, a Scot. He could board a train, but then he's reminded that the steam engine was invented by James Watt, another Scot. 'He has now been reminded too much of Scotland,' the tea towel proudly proclaims, 'and in desperation he picks up the Bible only to find that the first man mentioned in the good book is a Scot, King James VI, who authorised its translation.' The tea towel continues in a similar vein, until I'm filled with national pride. Or, at least, until the dishes are dry.

It's a material reminder of the power of national pride to lose any sense of perspective. James Watt invented a more practical steam engine, but he didn't start from scratch. His engine was based on the Newcomen engine (and Thomas Newcomen was English). Watt was able to improve the Newcomen engine because of a new drilling machine, which was invented by John Wilkinson (who was English). And, throughout the process, Watt collaborated with Matthew Boulton (who was English). It may also be true that the pneumatic tyre was invented by a Scot, but the car wasn't. It was invented by Carl Benz (who was German). Benz didn't start from scratch, of course, any more than Watt did. His automobile was based on all sorts of developments in other countries, such as the first steam road locomotive, which was invented by Richard Trevithick (who was English). And it may be true that, if you open a King James Bible, you'll see the name of King James. However, it's not as if he wrote the Bible. He merely had it translated (into English).

All of these inventions were based on earlier ideas and inventions, which were produced by people in other countries, and they've all been improved upon since. By people in other countries. There are obviously countless more inventions, and who, precisely, should get the credit has often been a matter of controversy among historians of science and technology. In the midst of all this, there have been many inventive folk who were born in Scotland. That's a fine thing. However, it doesn't make me special simply because I was also born here. Not to mention that anyone who knows any history might notice that there are some people missing. For example, the tea towel doesn't include the Scots who made fortunes from the slave trade, or from smuggling opium into China, or who were responsible for the massacre of indigenous people in Australia.

We can remember the past in various ways, and the way that we do shapes how we see ourselves. We can remember what individual Scots have done, or how we've cooperated with the English. Both are true enough, but what's made relevant paints a particular picture. The picture that's painted by the tea towel isn't subtle. Its title is: 'Wha's Like Us – Damn Few And They're A' Deid' (a condescending translation: 'Who is like us – hardly anyone and they are all deceased'). It's a picture of the Scots as exceptional. Throughout history, many nations have seen themselves as exceptional. This has rarely turned out well for others.

Nevertheless, it's one of our habits. We identify with *our* people: the people *here*. But where is here? After all, to Glaswegians, *here* is the East. To Highlanders, it's the South. To the English, it's the North. To most of the world, it's the West. Meanwhile, wherever we are, we experience the world as if we're at the centre of it all. As we look out, we quickly identify with those who seem to resemble us. It's another one of our habits: we distinguish between people in terms of in-groups and out-groups. We draw boundaries between us and them. We're Scottish not English. We're British not European. There are countless boundaries that might be drawn. Each discriminates in a different way. North. South. East. West. However, we take some for granted.

We assume that these boundaries mark a natural division even though, over time, they've shifted. Wherever the fuzzy boundary might be, however, we tend to remain loyal to the centre. At the heart of the matter is a basic assumption that we make about who we are. We're Scottish not English. We're British not European. This is preserved through history and heroes. They represent our national identity. But national identity, like all forms of identity, is created in contrast with others. It's typically a neighbour with whom we have a past, and how that past is told shapes how we see ourselves. Some of the people who tell us about that past aren't interested in the bigger picture. They direct our attention to this not that. Some of them focus on national heroes as if there are no national villains. Or, perhaps more fundamentally, as if there are heroes and villains.

Some insight into whom we think are the heroes was revealed in 2002, in a national poll of *100 Greatest Britons*. The highest Scot was Alexander Fleming, who discovered penicillin. He came in at number twenty, just below Paul McCartney, who was just below Queen Victoria, who was just below the actor and singer Michael Crawford. David Hume didn't make the top 100, but

David Beckham did. There were thirteen women. There were no black Britons. They had to make a separate programme: *100 Great Black Britons*. In many ways, the poll was absurd, but the winner was hardly surprising. It was Winston Churchill, who was a racist.

That depends, of course, on what we mean by 'racist'. In the recent protests about statues erected to slavers and racists in various countries, Churchill's name was brought up. Defenders of national pride leapt to his defence. They pointed out that this was the old normal, that a handful of quotes had been cherry-picked from an enormous number of books and speeches, and that many were second-hand quotes. They argued that he was against racial segregation in the United States, apartheid in South Africa and, of course, that he (if not single-handedly) defeated the Nazis. They didn't deny that he expressed racist views. But that, they pointed out, wasn't why he was a hero.

In the United States, there have been heated arguments about statues of George Washington, Thomas Jefferson, and even Abraham Lincoln. Is there anyone left in whom we can believe? Sacred cows are under attack, and are being defended, for what they represent. For some, they represent a racist legacy, which many people find offensive. For others, they represent national pride, and, for those people, the accusations of racism are offensive.

The statues represent different things to us, because no person is just one thing. We place them into one category or another, which represents only one thing about them. Which one is relevant depends on the context. He said racist things. He fought racist things. Heroes and villains, regardless of context, are mythical creatures that can only be seen when we look at them through the window of faith.

National pride is a kind of faith. But faith in what? It's based on a particular picture of here: the bits that we find appealing. We notice our heroes, not our villains. We notice the good things that they did, not the bad things. We're encouraged to take pride in this particular picture, which makes us seem exceptional. We sing our anthems, and wave our flags, and think that this is who we are.

But we're not exceptional. Every nation does this. Every nation celebrates their heroes and takes pride in the good things that they did. Every nation has villains too, and none of their heroes was perfect. And, in every nation, they erect statues to their heroes. Wherever we happen to be, the things that we take for granted about ourselves and others, or about our own history and heroes, shape who we think we are. And, in turn, this shapes our thoughts. We draw boundaries between us and them. We identify with a particular picture, which makes us think that we're special.

However, we can be more discriminating. We can admire some people from here – but only some of them. We can admire some things that they did – but only some of them. Our heroes and nations are imperfect. If we can't see their flaws, then we're not paying attention. However, at the same time, if we can't see their merits, then we're not paying attention – so, we can condemn some things that they did, but only some of them. Alternatively, if we wish to identify with something, then we could look beyond the assumptions that we make about others, and identify with what we really think. This, in the end, is who we are.

Whatever we think, it's based on assumptions. The assumptions that we make are shaped by our experience, which depends on the time and place in which we live. We follow our own traditions, and we stick to our familiar conventions. We have our particular customs

Radical Thinking

and habits. In the process, we tend to assume that what's normal, here and now, is obvious.

So, to see the bigger picture, we need to look beyond the here and now.

From here, I can see local reminders of how our assumptions are shaped by the here and now.

I can see the clock on the spire of the Tron Kirk, the former church down the road. For more than two centuries, it was the focus of the annual Hogmanay celebrations, when Edinburgh locals joined together to bring in the new year as it marked the stroke of midnight. Out with the old. In with the new. As 1811 became 1812, New Town residents came to the Tron to take part in the traditional celebration. They were attacked by Old Town gangs, who now saw them as wealthy outsiders. Old versus new. Insider versus outsider. The boundaries that we draw to mark time and space. They matter.

They matter here and now. It's time to head back to the office.

I'm passing the statue of Greyfriars Bobby again, which represents his loyalty. It's another long-standing tradition: we admire a loyal and faithful servant. Bobby was faithful to his master. Or so the tradition goes. However, the facts have long been questioned, and it's quite possible that the man whose grave he so faithfully attended was actually a stranger.[13] Nevertheless, a faithful dog was what a dog was supposed to be. This is why the generic name for a dog, not so long ago, was Fido. It was the name of Abraham Lincoln's dog, until 1865, when Lincoln was assassinated. And then, in 1866, Fido was assassinated. Having been conditioned to trust in strangers, he licked the face of a sleeping drunk: the drunk awoke, thought that he was being attacked, and stabbed poor old Fido.[14] So much for trusting in strangers.

But when nothing is certain and anything is possible, we need to rely on trust. We need to have faith in someone or something. We need to believe that the sun will rise tomorrow, at the expected time and place. We need to take some things for granted, because we live in the here and now. As we do, it all seems natural, but there's little that's natural about the ways in which we experience the here and now.

At the time of Hume, for example, most people lived in rural areas. Their work was seasonal and hours were variable, in between sunrise and sunset, because they earned their living by what they produced, not by how long they spent on it. This seemed natural, until the factory appeared. In order to maximise the use of the factory, workers were employed around the clock. They were paid for shifts, based on time not produce. Factory clocks and horns announced when it was time to start and end work. The experience of work was different now, as work time was separated from leisure time.[15]

Time became a currency. Time was money: it could be spent or spared or wasted. The introduction of the railways created the need for a national timetable, along with the opportunity for holidays (at appropriate times, when folk could get off work). We gradually became more clockwise, working Monday to Friday, nine till five, with days divided up according to various diaries, schedules and timetables. This came to seem natural, until we forgot that, for most of history, it was nothing like this.

The experience of space was slowly transformed as populations increased and migrated. Towns and cities grew in size and people

Radical Thinking

lived in more crowded conditions. This changed the sights and sounds and tastes and, yes, the smells that surrounded them. It changed how people thought and felt about others, and how they interacted with them. New forms of transport permitted folk to travel beyond their local space, to other regions, towns and cities, and then to other countries. New forms of communications put them in touch with folk from other parts of the world. We crossed the seas, flew over the mountains, and finally reached the moon. And, on the way there, we turned around and saw our little planet looking back. There were no national boundaries to see with our own eyes. Just a wee marble floating through space. And we realised that we were all astronauts now.

Or, perhaps, we were lost in space. Now we feel lost in a virtual space of endless and unreliable information, unable to trust in the things that we read and hear, or in the people who inform us. We rely on virtual spaces for information and don't have the time to check everything. We're busy people with places to go, and we don't have time for everyone. The ways that we interact with each other continue to be determined by the spaces in which we live, and by the time that we have to do it. Today, we're connected in ways that Hume would have thought impossible. However, to us, it all seems natural. But it's not natural. It's where we are now. We've conformed to new customs and habits.

Until, of course, a new normal appears.

This is hard to notice – unless it happens suddenly. If that were to happen, then we could compare the two and spot the differences. The experience of work would be different now, and so would the experience of time and space. We'd miss the old routines – but only some of them. We'd realise that certain people – for example, cleaners, shop workers, delivery drivers – were more important than we used to think. We might think that it was time to reconsider our priorities, because the things that we used to take for granted were no longer obvious. We might believe that it was time to change things.

But would we *really* believe that? After all, some people rub Hume's toe, or spit on the Heart of Midlothian, because they believe that it will bring good luck. But many do it because it's a local custom. They don't *really* believe. If we really think that it's time to change things, then we need to change things. Otherwise, we're merely conforming to new habits until we return to the good old days. And then we'll carry on as normal, back into the old routines, the familiar ways and beliefs that will once again seem as natural as the sun rising in the morning. We'll take the here and now for granted, and think that this is set in stone.

But it's not. As we see the sun rise every day – at the usual time and place – we might remember that it's actually our planet that's revolving, and that the time depends on the place in which we happen to be.

So, here and now, what do we do?

If nothing is certain and anything is possible, this doesn't mean that anything goes. It's just that we can't be certain. We need to take some things for granted in order to get stuff done. The assumptions we make are shaped by our experience. We have different experiences, and we make different assumptions. As we do, we draw different boundaries in space and time, and between us and them.

For centuries, we've lived by the clock and the calendar, which have measured time differently at different times and places. We

Radical Thinking

live in spaces defined by maps that represent them in different ways, some of which include different time zones. Wherever and whenever we might *really* be, we understand our 'here and now' in relation to there and then. We draw our boundaries and agree on what they mean. And then we take them for granted.

According to physics, space and time are relative, and time may be an illusion. Nevertheless, we – including physicists – set our clocks and fill our diaries, travel on scheduled trains and planes, and meet at agreed times and places. In the absence of absolute truth, we've come up with rules. At different times and in different places, we've come up with different rules. There have been different numbers of months in the year, days in the month, and days in the week. According to the rules, here and now, it's Saturday evening at eleven o'clock. In Sydney, however, it's Sunday morning and the sun has already risen on next week. Nevertheless, if we agree on the rules – according to these local customs and habits – then we can make plans and, most of the time, we can take them for granted. It's only when we encounter different rules – when the clocks are moved forward, or if we fly from here to Sydney, or if we read about the history of the calendar – that we're reminded of the existence of these rules.

We rarely notice the assumptions we make – the rules that we follow – that separate the 'here and now' from there and then. It just seems obvious to us. However, it's not obvious to others. And, when we encounter a different context, one in which the rules seem alien, it becomes obvious to us as well. A new normal is a useful reminder of the things that we take for granted.

Things change over time, and they're different elsewhere. The men who built the Radical Road knew this. They were inspired by the French Revolution and by the American War of Independence. They saw that radical change had happened elsewhere and believed that it could happen here. They challenged local customs and habits, because they could see the bigger picture. However, they wanted only men to be able to vote because, at that time, they took other things for granted.

So, we need to think about what we're missing. For example, as I walk around Edinburgh, I see countless statues. They are of philosophers (such as David Hume), of scientists (such as James Clerk Maxwell), of preachers (such as David Livingstone), of national heroes (such as William Wallace), and of writers (such as Walter Scott). There are several statues of monarchs and aristocrats, some of whom never set foot in the city. There's an impressive monument to Horatio Nelson, who never set foot in the city. There's even a statue of Abraham Lincoln, who never set foot in the country.

There are statues of fictional characters (such as Sherlock Holmes), who never set foot in the real world. There are also several statues of dogs. For example, the statues of Maxwell and Scott are accompanied by statues of their dogs, and there are statues solely dedicated to dogs. There's Greyfriars Bobby and, below the castle, there's a statue of Bum: a dog from San Diego, who never lifted a leg in the city. In the city centre, there are more statues dedicated to dogs and fictional characters than there are to women.[16]

As I walk these streets, I'm surrounded by representatives of inherited wealth and political power, religious faith and national pride, male ingenuity and loyal dogs. This is hardly the best representation of who we are. This, of course, can easily change. For example, we can erect more statues to women. It's not as if there aren't options. There are philosophers (such as Mary Shepherd),

Radical Thinking

scientists (such as Doris Reynolds), preachers (such as May Drummond), national heroes (such as Elsie Inglis) and writers (such as Muriel Spark). There are female saints and sinners.[17]

But no woman represents just one thing. If we assume that an individual who fits into *that* category is deserving of a statue, then we might miss the bigger picture. For example, one of the daughters of Edinburgh who has been suggested is Marie Stopes, the pioneer of birth control.[18] However, her views about 'racial purity', and about the potential of birth control to improve 'racial progress', are harder to admire.[19]

So, we need to decide on the rules. More women. Fewer racists. That seems fair enough. And then what? Another suggestion has been J. K. Rowling, bestselling author and philanthropist, though also a woman whose views about 'women' have offended a number of people (which prompted a number of offensive responses). As we discussed in Chapter 3, words, and what they represent, can change. They can mean different things to different people. So, as we engage with alternative views – about what it means to be a 'woman', or a 'man', or anything else – we're bound to draw different boundaries.

But we need to remember that, when we draw different boundaries, we cross other lines. As I walk back, I cross Chambers Street, which was part of a Victorian reshaping of Edinburgh: in the process, older squares and buildings were demolished. As I walk back farther, just before I enter George Square, I pass the Rhino Head sculpture. It marks the former site of the Paperback Bookshop (which used to have a rhino head hanging outside). In 1960, it made the news when a copy of *Lady Chatterley's Lover* was publicly burned here. It was considered offensive.

We've demolished buildings and squares. We've burned books.

When we draw different boundaries, we cross other lines. However, it needn't be so destructive. We just need to decide on the rules. We can be Scottish and/or British and/or European. We can be men and/or women and/or other. We can be many kinds of people.

But when we draw boundaries, we create divisions. We then take sides and, in the process, we create new identities: we are us, not them. We take these categories for granted. However, no person is just one thing. Depending on the particular boundary that we draw, the person might be on our side, or on the other side. According to one boundary, they're one of us. According to another boundary, they're one of them.

As individuals, of course, we can set our own boundaries. We can stay within them, feeling in control, because things feel safe and familiar here. But we can't prevent others from doing the same. At some point, *their* boundaries will cross *our* lines. This can seem like a problem. Or a threat. But it's neither. This is an opportunity.

We make assumptions about ourselves and others: about what they're like, and how we're different. We *define* ourselves in contrast with others. They help us to understand who *we* are. We're us not them. We think this, they think that. We identify with different positions. However, we all got there through a similar process.

So, we can think about the process, not the outcome. We all make certain assumptions, draw our own boundaries, and follow our own rules. We then take them for granted, as if they're natural … until we encounter a new normal. That's when we realise that other lines can be drawn, and that the rules might be different. That's when we notice the assumptions that *we* have been making, which shape our own thoughts. And this is an opportunity: it's a reminder of our own limits.

If we wish to see the bigger picture, then we need to engage with alternative perspectives. But we need to decide on the rules. These, of course, are of our own making, but they'll only work if we reach some kind of consensus. Our heroes are bound to be villains to others. The views of some are bound to offend us. But we used to hang sinners. We enslaved the other. We burned offensive books. We now send offensive tweets. That, at least, is a degree of progress. And the debate will continue, because we'll not agree on everything. However, the rules of the debate are up to us.

If we shout at each other, then we'll talk past each other. We'll not hear what *they* are really saying. When we argue about saints and sinners, we're often arguing about good and bad ideas. We can, and should, argue about what we think are good or bad ideas. However, if we think in terms of goodies and baddies, then we'll be missing the point. We need to get into the habit of drawing a different boundary: between the idea and the individual. If we agree on the topic in dispute, at least, this provides a kind of consensus. And, as we'll see later, in terms of critical thinking, this is essential.

Meanwhile, if we take it for granted that we're right (and they're wrong), that we're the goodies (and they're the baddies), that our voices must be heard (and theirs must be silenced), then we're heading back to the good old days of persecution and intolerance. We used to hang folk for expressing offensive beliefs. From a historical perspective, we've made progress. But in recent years, it's been getting worse. Here and now, we're heading in the wrong direction.

I've now walked back to where I was before.

* * *

Local customs and habits

We look at the world through a local window.

Whatever we think, it's based on our experience – on what we notice and how we interpret it – but our experience is always limited. We can't, therefore, be certain of anything. So, in order to get by, we make assumptions – based on *our* local picture – about the bigger picture. On the basis of our experience, we draw particular boundaries, and come up with particular rules.

However, these foundations aren't set in stone. They're local customs and habits that, in an uncertain world, provide some guidance. They suggest particular ways of thinking. They present particular heroes and villains. They help us to make sense of our time and place by making *this* context seem natural. We accept this because we prefer the familiar, which is easier to process than the unfamiliar. And, when we encounter people who see things differently, we wonder why *they* think *that*?

It's easy to doubt the unfamiliar. It's harder to doubt what we take for granted. However, if we wish to understand, then it's simple: we just need to listen to what *they* are saying until we understand what they mean by *that*. They may have different rules, draw different boundaries, and recognise different heroes and villains. But that's not a problem. We needn't agree with them. We can use this to remind us of our own limits.

If we listen.

Of course, they'll try to persuade you. They'll describe the facts – but only some of them. They'll do this in ways that are designed to convince you. They'll make particular things relevant. They'll make them appealing so that you go along with them. They'll use the tools of persuasion in the real-world practice of *make-believe*.

So, it's time to consider these tools.

6

Tools of persuasion

'Edinburgh has been greatly agitated by a delusion,' Professor Bennett of the University announced in 1851. It seemed to be affecting everyone in town. 'Noblemen, members of the learned professions, and respectable citizens,' he explained, 'have been amusing themselves in private' and 'sensitive ladies do not object to indulge in the emotions so occasioned.' Meanwhile, 'girls and boys throw themselves into states of trance and ecstasy … for the amusement of their companions.' Worst of all, 'students in this university have [been] obliged, from want of attention and mental power, to absent themselves from their classes.'[1]

Professor Bennett called it 'The Mesmeric Mania of 1851'. He explained that it had now spread beyond Edinburgh, had 'appeared in many towns of Scotland' and was currently in 'London, where, according to the papers, there are at present repeated the same public scenes'.[2] All of this recent agitation, he explained, had been caused by visiting Americans. They'd been giving public performances, for the price of a shilling, which had led to a delusion. The delusion was this: 'that certain persons may be influenced by an external mysterious force'.[3]

It's a local lesson in how our thoughts are shaped not by some mysterious force, but by what other people tell us.

The visiting Americans were travelling showmen who were demonstrating the latest version of 'mesmerism' (named after Franz Mesmer, who had called the mysterious force 'animal magnetism'). In this new version, volunteers were instructed to gaze at a small coin in the palm of their hand for a few minutes. This created a 'peculiar' mental condition. They could then be prevented from opening their mouths or bending their arms, from standing up or sitting down, and could be made 'to walk, dance, or run, as directed; to imitate riding on horseback, when seated on a chair; or stagger about the room in a supposed state of intoxication'.[4]

Having witnessed these public exhibitions, many people had decided to try it at home. This is what had led to respectable gentlemen and sensitive ladies in Edinburgh amusing themselves in private, children throwing themselves into states of trance and ecstasy, and students absenting themselves from classes. As far as Professor Bennett was concerned, this delusion about a mysterious force was having a very bad influence.

There was, however, nothing new about this. Throughout the early nineteenth century, mesmerists had been travelling from country to country, and from city to city, to show how the mysterious force of 'mesmerism' (or 'animal magnetism') could be used to manipulate what people thought, how they felt, and what they did. They'd placed their subjects into a trance state so that they couldn't be awoken, even when bottles of ammonia were waved beneath their nostrils. They'd made their subjects insensible to pain, even while having their teeth extracted, or when having a limb amputated.

Radical Thinking

And many had claimed to be cured of illness by the mysterious force of mesmerism.

These events had been observed and reported. Believers in mesmerism had cited them as facts. However, disbelievers hadn't been persuaded, because they'd interpreted what they saw and heard in a different way. When they'd seen a subject in a trance state, they'd claimed that she was faking it. When they'd read that a patient reported feeling no pain as his leg was being amputated, they'd claimed that the patient was lying. And, when the well-known writer Harriet Martineau announced that she'd been cured of a uterine disease by mesmerism, they'd said that she was 'hysterical'. This had been the view of Sir Benjamin Brodie, President of the Royal College of Surgeons. It had also been the view of Charles Darwin, who'd noted that a 'tendency to deceive is characteristic of disordered females'.[5]

In the midst of the controversy, the Scottish surgeon James Braid had been more discriminating. He'd tried to persuade both believers and disbelievers that they'd got it wrong — but only some of it. According to him, the facts were facts, but the theory of 'animal magnetism' was false. Trances could be induced — that part was true — but not by a mysterious force. It was caused by focusing the attention of subjects, which made their minds vulnerable to suggestion. Through focused attention and suggestion, Braid had explained, pain could also be reduced and (some) illnesses could be cured. He'd called his theory 'neurypnology'. Then he changed the name. It was now called 'hypnotism'.[6]

Professor Bennett had been persuaded by this. And so, in 1851, he explained to the deluded of Edinburgh that they could *not* be influenced by an 'external mysterious force'. How did he try to convince them? He told them that the people who claimed this were incompetent and dishonest.[7] He told them that, to a medical expert (such as him), the theory was so implausible as to 'scarcely merit attention'.[8] He told them that it was incompatible with science and that it was harmful to those who believed it.[9]

These mesmerists, he explained, were merely getting individuals to focus their attention, which made them suggestible. However, this could be avoided. If subjects refused to have their attention directed by the mesmerist, then they couldn't be influenced. They weren't at the mercy of a mysterious force: they were '*putting themselves*' (original italics) into a position of vulnerability.[10] At the end of the day, it was up to them.

Not everyone was persuaded by this. For example, William Gregory, another professor at the University of Edinburgh, had witnessed many demonstrations of mesmerism, including those of the recent Americans. He'd seen and heard things that, he felt, couldn't be explained by mere attention and suggestion. These included cases of miraculous cures, clairvoyance and precognition. In 1851, he published a large book that catalogued these strange phenomena. He did his best to persuade others that the mysterious force was real and that it could be used to influence people into thinking or feeling or doing all kinds of things. Given that his colleague had just said the opposite, how did he do that?

Professor Gregory explained that, unlike the disbelievers, he'd studied the subject fully. He displayed his credentials – 'M.D., F.R.S.E., Professor of Chemistry at the University of Edinburgh' – to show that he had scientific expertise. He was motivated not by 'irrational scepticism' but rather by a 'sincere love of truth'.[11] '[B]y diligent observation of the facts', he claimed, the laws of animal magnetism would be discovered, and these would account for the facts in the same way that scientific laws 'account for the facts of astronomy, electricity, heat, light, and magnetism proper'.[12] He pointed out that 'there has been a growing interest in it, in all quarters', that the phenomena of animal magnetism had now been 'repeatedly observed and produced by well-qualified experimenters' and that 'in the medical profession, there are many, who not only are convinced of the truth of Animal Magnetism, but actually use it ... as an appropriate means of cure'.[13]

In other words, he presented himself as honest and competent: as a reliable authority. He presented animal magnetism as plausible. He presented mesmeric treatment as something that was relevant and appealing. As the debate continued, believers (and, in response, disbelievers) would each try to persuade the public that they were honest and competent: that *they* were the reliable authorities. They would claim that such beliefs were plausible (or implausible), that mesmerism was important (or trivial), and that it was beneficial (or harmful).[14] They would do this because, if a reliable authority tells us something that seems plausible, relevant and appealing, then we tend to believe it.

Many people were persuaded to believe in the mysterious force of 'animal magnetism', or 'mesmerism', and its name continued to change. They went on to believe in a 'psychic' force, miraculous 'mind-cures', and 'New Thought', which claimed that there was a 'law of attraction' that governed this mysterious force. According to this 'law of attraction' (as described back in 1889): positive thoughts attract positive experiences and negative thoughts attract negative ones. Simply by thinking good thoughts, you could attract anything that you wanted: from happiness and health to personal wealth.

This nineteenth-century idea was appealing and became the core message of the self-help industry, which repeated it throughout the twentieth century.

It has continued to be repeated in this century, and it's still something that people find appealing. In 2006, the 'law of attraction' was (mysteriously) rebranded as a 'secret' in the bestselling book *The Secret*. Noblemen, members of the learned professions and respectable citizens read it in private, and ladies did not object to indulge in the emotions so occasioned. Millions were persuaded to buy the book, and some of them no doubt felt better. Meanwhile, disbelievers were greatly agitated by the delusion about a mysterious force that somehow continued to be a bad influence.

However, it wasn't the force that was having the influence. It was those who were selling the idea. They presented themselves as reliable authorities. They presented the idea as plausible. They made it seem relevant and appealing. They did the things that people do when they wish to persuade you of something.

People can be influenced in many ways. For over a century, psychologists have studied this. They've given it names. They've come up with rules. In the real world, however, what names mean, and how rules are applied, depend on the context. So, there have been different names, with different meanings, and different sets of rules, which have been applied in different ways.

Psychologists rejected the claims of mesmerism, but many accepted the claims of hypnotism. That meant, according to its original meaning: by fixing the attention of the subject, a special hypnotic state could be produced. But this was also controversial. There were ongoing disputes about whether the hypnotic state was normal or abnormal, about whether it revealed an alternate personality, and even about whether there was a special hypnotic state.

Whatever they thought about hypnotism, however, psychologists became increasingly convinced that 'suggestion' was fundamental to how we think, feel and behave. In the early twentieth century, it became a way of understanding almost everything that people thought, felt and did. But what was 'suggestion'? It meant all kinds of things. It was both 'passive' and 'active', 'conscious' and 'unconscious' (and, at times, it was 'incompletely conscious'). It was a mental phenomenon or an emotional phenomenon. Or both. Sometimes, it appeared to cover 'practically all conscious and unconscious cognitive and affective processes'.[15]

As it seemed to cover everything, it could apparently influence what people noticed, how they interpreted it, what they remembered, what they believed, and what they wanted. Whatever 'suggestion' was, then, it would be useful to know how it worked in the real world. If only they could figure out the rules. And, before long, they came up with some rules. Before the First World War, the American psychologist Harry Hollingworth was advising would-be persuaders to adhere to certain rules. He called them the 'laws of suggestion': get their attention, communicate a single idea, repeat it, make it clear, repeat it, make it positive, make it relevant to them, and ensure that it comes from a source of authority.[16]

Suggestion, based on rules such as these, was used in advertising and in propaganda. It was now considered a more effective means of persuasion than rational argument and evidence. It was used to shape American opinion towards entering the First World War (by stoking xenophobia) and during the war (to maintain public morale and to reinforce xenophobia). After the war, however, the obvious power of propaganda began to worry people. The public appeared to be *too* easily persuaded. They were highly suggestible, accepting of prejudice, and vulnerable to 'radical' ideas. In the 1920s and 1930s, the dangers of fascist and communist propaganda, of widespread prejudice and gullibility, were becoming increasingly obvious. American psychologists and educators, like many others, wanted to do something about this.

So, in March of 1937, a group met in Boston for a meeting on 'Education for Democracy'.[17] It included a selection of experts on persuasion, such as Freud's nephew Edward Bernays, the 'inventor' of Public Relations. It also included Alfred Adler, the psychologist who had written about the 'inferiority complex'. He had been President of the Vienna Psychoanalytic Society, and the first major figure to leave it (because he disagreed with Freud's ideas). In the next few weeks, it was agreed to set up an anti-propaganda institute. As it happens, Bernays wouldn't be part of it (he felt that propaganda was essential in a democracy). Neither would Adler (he would be dead). In May of that year, he was visiting Scotland when he died suddenly. He was cremated in Edinburgh.

Nevertheless, a few months later, the Institute for Propaganda Analysis was founded in New York. In their new bulletin, *Propaganda Analysis*, the Institute published an article entitled 'How to Detect Propaganda'. They reckoned that, if American citizens were more aware of how propaganda worked, then they wouldn't be so easily persuaded. The article described another set of rules: the 'seven common propaganda devices'. The seven devices worked because 'they appeal to our emotions rather than to our reason'.[18]

According to the Institute for Propaganda Analysis, these are the things that persuade us.

Radical Thinking

The first of the propaganda devices was *Name-calling*: the propagandist used 'bad names' to refer to certain people and things (which made them easier to reject). In 1930s America, 'bad names' included 'communist', 'heretic' and 'alien'. That was almost a century ago, of course, when communists, non-Christians and immigrants were considered un-American. Back then, claiming that a politician was not *really* American could be effective. Particularly if this was repeated over and over again. Repetition is a basic technique in propaganda.

The second device was called *Glittering Generalities*: the propagandist used 'virtue words' with no specific meaning (which made them easier to accept). In 1930s America, politicians would claim to be defenders of 'the Constitution', of 'freedom', and of 'the American way'. Whatever that meant, it was obviously a good thing. A critic of Roosevelt once declared that it was the entrepreneurial spirit that would 'make America great again'.[19] Back then, they thought that would work, but he should have said it more than once. Glittering generalities need to be repeated, over and over again, because repetition is a basic technique in propaganda.

The third device was called *Transfer*: the propagandist associated their position with something that was revered. In 1930s America, politicians praised God, quoted the parts of Scripture that suited them, and wrapped themselves in the flag. Back then, they hoped to benefit from the association. God Bless America, God Bless America, repeated over and over again, because repetition is a basic technique in propaganda.

The fourth device was called *Testimonial*: the propagandist supported their position by using testimonials from others. In 1930s America, the testimonials of business owners, preachers and celebrities were used to endorse political candidates. Back then, this was thought to work. Since then, candidates have been endorsed by Frank Sinatra, Marilyn Monroe, Paul Newman and Stephen Baldwin.

The fifth device was *Plain Folks*: the propagandist pretended to be ordinary (so that they appeared to be one of the people). In 1930s America, politicians seeking election would present themselves as regular folks. Back then, they'd be photographed at home, or in church, or while engaging in everyday American activities such as throwing a baseball or carrying a gun.

The sixth device was *Card-stacking*: the propagandist would often exaggerate, conceal and distort the facts. In 1930s America, politicians would often exaggerate, conceal and distort the facts. Back then, they would indulge in 'sham' and 'hypocrisy' to 'make the unreal appear real and the real appear unreal'.[20] They might do this repeatedly, over and over again, because repetition is a basic technique in propaganda.

The seventh and final device was *Bandwagon*: the propagandist presented their position as popular (so that others would 'follow the crowd'). In 1930s America, politicians would fill a large stadium and put on a spectacle with music and lights to attract as large an audience as possible.[21] They'd pretend to be more popular than they were. They might do this over and over again, because – and this isn't said often enough – repetition is a basic technique in propaganda.

These techniques, according to the Institute for Propaganda Analysis in 1937, are the things that persuade us. 'We are fooled by propaganda,' they explained, 'chiefly because we don't recognize it when we see it.' They believed that, if we knew about these techniques, then we would 'more easily recognize propaganda when we

Radical Thinking

see it'.[22] In 1937, people hadn't known how propaganda worked but, now that they knew the rules, this would diminish the power of propaganda. And that worked out just fine.

The same techniques are clearly recognisable today. They continue to be cited as common propaganda techniques. That's because they continue to be used. That's because they continue to work. They continue to work because describing opponents in a negative way, appealing to vague positive concepts, associating yourself with revered institutions, being supported by others, appearing to be one of the people, spinning the facts, and claiming to be popular, can always work. And learning the names of seven general ways in which we can be persuaded won't prevent this. After all, there are more than seven ways. For example, the seven devices didn't include repetition, which is a basic technique in propaganda.

The problem with these lists of 'rules' and 'devices' is that they're inadequate. They're abstract concepts taken out of context. In the real world, persuasion happens in a context. It's based on particular arguments that are designed for particular audiences. Whether we even recognise a so-called 'device' will depend on how it's done. And whether we believe what we're told will depend on what they actually tell us, on whether we trust the source, on what we already believe, and on what we want to hear.

Meanwhile, there are different kinds of persuasion. Every argument is an attempt to persuade. The last sentence was an attempt to persuade. Persuasion is used by philosophers and scientists. It can be used to educate as well as to manipulate. It can be used with different objectives in mind. It isn't necessarily a bad thing. It depends on the objective. The difference between 'propaganda' and 'education' is often a matter of objectives.

To persuade people to think like we do. To persuade people to think for themselves.

The following year, the Institute for Propaganda Analysis published something else: the first 'Critical Thinking' test.

The authors felt that, in the battle against propaganda, the key weapon was education. The aim of propaganda was to persuade people to think in certain ways. The aim of education was also to persuade people to think in certain ways. However, as far as the authors were concerned, the former was based on emotion and prejudice. The latter, in terms of critical thinking, was based on logic and evidence. This, they felt, was better: it would help students to think for themselves. To make this work, they had to come up with a way to assess what kind of teaching instilled the methods of critical thinking. They had to measure the critical thinking ability of students, before and after a series of lessons, to see if this led to improvement.

To measure anything, you need to get numbers. To measure anything that's in the mind, you need to get people to do something that you can observe. Something that can be counted. Carry out a task. Fill in a questionnaire. Complete a test. Something with a score. The results provide numerical data, and then sets of data can be compared. This group versus that group. Before versus after. On that basis, psychologists can say that men and women, or old and young, or extraverts and introverts, or them and us, differ in a particular way. They can say that, after something happens, something else increases or decreases. In this case, teaching would happen and, hopefully, 'critical thinking' would increase.

But first, they had to measure 'critical thinking', and that meant getting numbers. They had to get people to do something that

Radical Thinking

represented 'critical thinking' – and a specific amount of it. To do this, they asked a number of questions, the answers to which were either right or wrong. The correct answers represented 'critical thinking'. Incorrect answers represented a lack of it. They couldn't rely on general knowledge because 'critical thinking' was supposed to be a general ability which was independent of factual knowledge.

So, the questions that they came up with were logical and self-contained. They were based on the rules of logic. They contained all the relevant information and all of this could be assumed to be true. Here's an example from the original test, which tests logical reasoning:

> All patriotic people are to be admired.
> No radicals are patriotic people.
> Therefore –
>   A. No radicals are to be admired.
>   B. All radicals are to be admired.
>   C. Some radicals are to be admired.
>   D. None of these conclusions necessarily follows.[23]

With the rules fixed, and the facts known, there was an obvious correct answer. If you understood the rules of logic. And, if you're curious what the correct answer is, then we'll get to this (and the rules of logic) later.[24] Meanwhile, in terms of this measure of 'critical thinking', the initial statements ('All patriotic people are to be admired' and 'No radicals are patriotic people') were *assumed* to be true. It was then up to the students to figure out the correct answer by using their 'critical thinking' ability. They weren't supposed to question these assumptions. They merely had to get the answer right, regardless of how they got there. 'Critical thinking', when it was measured, was based on the outcome, not the process.

Having come up with a way to measure 'critical thinking', psychologists now had to decide what teaching might increase it. Since critical thinking was, as far as they were concerned, largely a matter of logic, this was an obvious topic. So, they put together a series of lessons, which included several lessons in logic. They measured students before and after. They also measured other students, who didn't take these lessons, as a control group. The results were positive, if not surprising: the students who had taken the lessons (which were largely based on logic) showed greater improvement in 'critical thinking' (which was largely based on logic).[25]

This, in itself, was no bad thing. And, if 'critical thinking' is 'logical thinking' (which is how it's often been defined), then that's grand. However, this kind of 'critical thinking' has its limits. In the real world, for example, we can't assume that 'All patriotic people are to be admired'. After all, most racists are patriotic. We can't assume that 'No radicals are patriotic people'. After all, 'radicals' who fought for the right to vote also fought for our country.[26] In the real world, we can't assume that any statement is true.

However, people may try to persuade us that they're 'patriotic' and that others aren't. They may try to persuade us that 'radical' thinking is dangerous and not to be admired. They may try to persuade us to believe this and to want that. They may or may not use logic and evidence. But, even if they do, they'll do other things too. They'll present themselves as honest and competent. They'll present their own views as plausible. They'll make them seem relevant and appealing. They may do this whether they're right or wrong. They may do it to achieve different objectives. To inform. To sell. To manipulate. Education. Advertising. Propaganda.

If we wish to think in a critical way – if we wish to think for ourselves – then we need to think about the bigger picture. It's not just a matter of right or wrong. Logic and evidence may help us to distinguish between good and bad arguments. However, they don't distinguish between good and bad objectives. If the objective is to persuade us to buy *this*, or to vote for *them*, then this is also relevant. What they say may be true, but it will still present a *particular* picture.

If we don't understand the context, then we won't understand the agenda.

Psychologists have described all manner of ways in which we can be persuaded. At the start of the twentieth century, persuasion was seen in terms of 'suggestion', which meant all sorts of things. The so-called 'laws of suggestion', like the 'seven propaganda devices', were merely a few common themes. However, they made different themes relevant. Make it positive or use bad names. Be an authority or one of the people. Make it clear or keep it vague. All of these can work, depending on the context.

We can be persuaded by a positive message and by negative name-calling, by someone who is an authority and by someone who seems to be one of us. We can be persuaded by hearing a clear message, so clear and simple that it's extremely vague. *We can do this. Yes, we can.* But whether it works will depend on the message, on what it means in a given situation, on who is saying it and whether we trust them, and on what we already believe and want.

The psychology of persuasion makes certain themes relevant, depending on the context. In the world of sales and advertising, for example, there have long been six or seven 'principles of persuasion'.[27] According to the principle of 'reciprocation', we're more likely to say 'yes' when we feel indebted to someone. So, we're offered free samples or advice to encourage us to buy further products or services. According to the principle of 'scarcity', we value things that are in limited supply. So, when we book a hotel online, we're told to grab a deal 'before it's too late' and that there are 'only 2 rooms left!' These are persuasive in the context of sales, but they're very different from the 'laws of suggestion' and the 'seven common propaganda devices'.

There are, of course, some common themes. For example, there's the principle of 'social proof' (we tend to do what others do). This is rather like the 'bandwagon' device (present your position as popular so that others want to follow the crowd). There are also the principles of 'liking' (we tend to agree with someone we like) and 'unity' (we tend to agree with someone we consider to be one of us).[28] The latter, in particular, is rather like the 'plain folks' device (appear to be like one of the people). There's also the principle of 'authority' (we tend to believe authorities). This was one of the 'laws of suggestion'. It overlaps with the 'testimonial' device (if the testimonial is from a source of authority) and with the 'transfer' device (if the audience reveres authorities).

However, we live in a world in which experts are increasingly being denounced. Who, now, are the authorities? Whose testimonials are now persuasive? Which institutions are now revered? Which crowd, of all the crowds that are available, are we inclined to follow? Who is, and why are they, likeable? After all, there have been leaders who are both loved and hated, yet this has worked out in their favour. They've been loved by the people who love them, in part because they've claimed to be hated by others.

When they've been called bad names, accused of indulging in glittering generalities, denounced by revered institutions and in the testimonials of others, accused of being privileged (not plain folks) and of exaggerating, concealing and distorting the facts, they've continued to be followed by their crowd. The more they've been hated, the more they've been loved, because all the facts have been interpreted in line with their side of the argument. When we see the world in terms of goodies and baddies, we no longer think for ourselves.

There is, of course, nothing new about this. But how it's done depends on the context, which makes *certain* things relevant. In the 1930s, the power of propaganda to persuade the public by exaggerating, concealing and distorting the facts, by calling *certain* people bad names, by appealing to *certain* revered institutions (for example, the greatness of 'the nation') and *certain* experts (who provided testimonials), by appealing to *certain* plain folks (but not all of them), and to *certain* vague generalities, people could be persuaded to believe the most extraordinary and dangerous things.

'The purpose of propaganda', according to one influential book of the time, was 'to attract public attention to *certain* things ... to create a general conviction regarding the reality of a *certain* fact [and of] the necessity of *certain* things' (my italics). It avoided alternative perspectives by presenting 'a systematically one-sided attitude'. And, of course, 'effective propaganda ... should be persistently repeated.' The book was called *Mein Kampf*.[29]

The same techniques continue to work because they're far from obvious. They're not obvious because they're used in particular ways: to appeal to certain people who notice, believe and want different things. They work, in different ways, in education, in advertising and sales, and in propaganda. In other words, there are endless ways in which we can be persuaded.

Nevertheless, psychologists now often categorise them into two kinds. According to 'dual process' models, there are two routes to being persuaded. One relies on mental shortcuts (for example, we believe someone who seems credible). The other is based on the quality of the argument (for example, logic and evidence). Unless we're able and willing to do so, we rely on mental shortcuts rather than on logic and evidence. This is in line with the general view that we think in one of two ways: we think in 'implicit' and 'explicit' ways (which are, respectively, 'fast' and 'slow').[30] In short, in terms of critical thinking, we need to take it slowly. We need to make it explicit.

If we take the time to consider a claim – the logic that it follows, the evidence in support of it, the plausibility of the claim, and the reliability of the source – then we can assess it better. These are rules, of a kind, like the 'laws of suggestion' or the 'seven propaganda devices'. They may be true but, like all rules, they're abstract. They need to be applied in a particular context. Is *this* logical? Does the evidence support *that*? Is *this* a reliable source for *that*? If we wish to think in a more critical way, even when we're dealing with logic and evidence, we need to think about context.

Our thoughts are shaped by what others tell us. As they tell us about things, they appeal to the facts, but only some of them, and present them in a particular way. They present themselves as reliable sources. They present what they say as plausible. They make it relevant. They make it appealing. Depending on the context, there are countless ways in which they might do this. And, depending on the context, they may have different objectives in mind.

So, we need to remember our limits. When something is consistent with our own beliefs, we find it more plausible. However, we can consider alternative perspectives. We're also drawn to what we think is relevant and what we find appealing. That's why, when others try to persuade us, they make what they say seem relevant and appealing. At the end of the day, though, it's still up to us.

The power of suggestion depends on attention. *We* can decide what we think is relevant. The tools of persuasion are aimed at the audience. They're directed to what appeals to *us*. They may rely on logic and evidence, but they also appeal to our emotions and desires. They try to convince us that *this* will make us feel better and that *this* is what we want. And some things, depending on how we feel and what we want, are easier to believe. However, it's still up to us: it depends on how we feel and what we want.

We can be directed by logic and evidence, or by appeals to our emotions and desires. In the real world, all of these are relevant. However, in terms of our emotions and desires, we can think about them in a more critical way. We can make them explicit.

How we feel. What we want. As we'll see, these are also things that shape our thoughts.

7

How we feel

I'm looking out of the window at George Square. I'm thinking: *that* is how I feel.

George Square was once on the margins of Edinburgh but, over time, it ended up in the centre. And *that* is how I feel: once on the margins, now in the centre. Once on the fringe of society, young and unemployed in Thatcher's Britain, sleeping on a mattress in a cupboard of a shared room, spending the dole money less on food than on things for which it was never intended. Now a respectable member of society, a good citizen who works for a living, pays his taxes and obeys the law.

I can see George Square Gardens. This was once open land. It's now surrounded by iron railings. The gates are locked outside working hours. Signs have been posted that warn not to do things. No Smoking. Keep Off the Grass. It has become increasingly restricted. And *that* is how I feel: more restricted. There are so many things that I used to do. But not any more. No Smoking. Keep Off the Grass.

I saw The Damned. I saw The Clash. I used to listen to Grandmaster Flash. I was there at the birth of punk and the birth of rap.

Radical Thinking

I was there. But now I'm here: once on the fringe but now in the centre. And more restricted.

I suppose I could try to appear to be younger. But George Square tried that. In the 1960s, many of the Georgian buildings were replaced with younger buildings. Compared to the simple, elegant originals that remain, they look a bit ridiculous. And *that* is how I feel. Part of me is still the old me but, if I attempted to look younger, then I'd look a bit ridiculous.

There was a time, of course, when I didn't care. I had pierced ears and dyed my hair. But much of my hair, like much of the original square, is now gone.

I feel like … George Square.

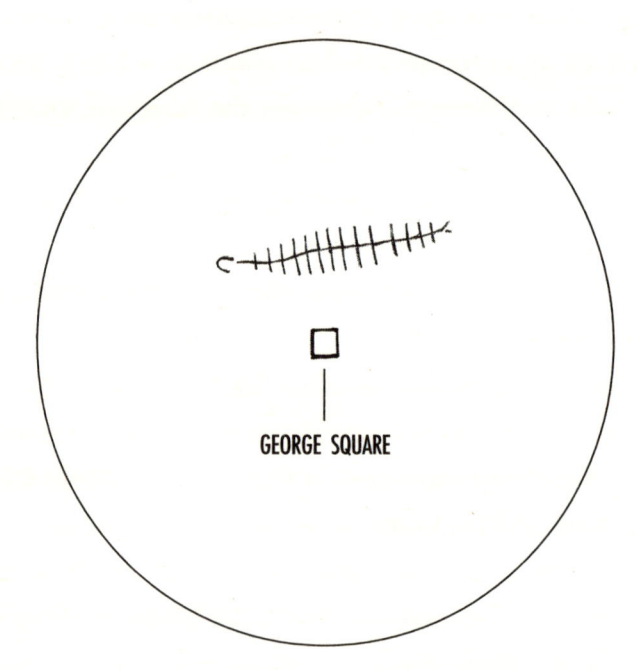

George Square, south of the fishbone-shaped High Street, was once on the fringe of Edinburgh, but now it's in the centre. If you look at it from a different perspective (upside down), then you can see how I feel.

How do *you* feel?

It seems like an easy question but, if you think about it, then the answer isn't so obvious. To describe our feelings, we need to use words to represent them. And we need words that others can understand, so that they know what we mean. But where can we find the words to convey how we *feel*?

We begin by looking outside, seeing something, and saying: I feel like *that*.

We look at the world, give names to things, and then we use those words to describe what's going on inside our heads. I feel 'fine' or 'rough'. I feel 'up' or 'down', 'high' or 'low', 'uplifted' or 'depressed'. I feel 'brilliant' or 'dim', 'buoyant' or 'deflated'. We rely on metaphors of external things (which can be seen) to understand internal feelings. That's what we did with 'emotion'. The word once referred to physical movement. Then we used it to refer to how we're internally moved.[1]

We fail to notice this because the meanings now seem obvious. We just feel 'happy', which took its meaning from a word that referred to good things happening. We just feel 'sad', which came from being sated, physically full, having had enough. We now know what we mean and we take it for granted. We even have emojis, which convey our feelings with cartoon faces and suggestive vegetables. However, before we use them – particularly those suggestive vegetables – we need to know what they mean.

We come up with ways to describe our feelings, and we agree on what they mean. We've done this, in different times and places, in very different ways. We don't notice this because, in *this* time and place, it isn't obvious. However, if we compare different contexts, then we can spot the differences. We can see that how we

Radical Thinking

understand our feelings – indeed, how we feel – is shaped by the time and place in which we live.

This, in turn, shapes our thoughts about how we feel, and how we want to feel.

I feel that a change of context might help.

I'm now walking down Nicolson Street, where *Encyclopaedia Britannica* first appeared, but I'm not sure about the exact address. This makes me feel uncertain. I'm walking past the Festival Theatre, the site of the old Empire Theatre, where Houdini once performed. This makes me feel nostalgic. I'm now at the entrance of Old College, once the main site of the University. Right now, this feels more relevant.

It's where, in 1785, James Hutton presented his radical view of our world as one that was constantly evolving through gradual ruin and reconstruction. By then, the university buildings had gradually evolved into 'a ruinous condition'.[2] So, a new building was constructed. It took a while, what with limited funds and the Napoleonic Wars, but, when it was finished, it was an architectural masterpiece that made people feel proud. At that time, it was called the New College. But that was two centuries ago. Today, it's called Old College. In any case, this is where, in the 1810s, as the new building was being constructed, 'the emotions' were invented.[3]

Until the eighteenth century, the word 'emotion' referred to physical movement. By 1810, it was a word that was used only occasionally to refer to human feelings. These were still better known, and had been for centuries, as the 'passions' and the 'affections'. These words referred to different kinds of feelings, which related to reason, will and morality in very different ways. The passions were seen as involuntary vices, which needed rational control. The affections, on the other hand, were movements of the rational part of the soul and were considered virtuous.

This changed when Thomas Brown proposed the modern concept of 'the emotions'. Brown was a philosopher at the University of Edinburgh who, in the 1810s, gave a series of lectures here. In these lectures, which were later published, he drew a new map of human feelings, based on particular similarities and differences.[4] He grouped the passions and the affections (and other kinds of feelings) into a single category: 'the emotions'. He also drew a new boundary that separated emotions from reason, will and morality. Emotions, as a whole, were now irrational things, out of control and lacking in principle.

Over the following decades, the emotions were described in all sorts of ways. Darwin wrote about the emotions of humans *and* animals in terms of evolutionary theory. According to him, emotions were biological. When triggered, they caused physiological changes that could be seen in bodily and facial expressions, such as a laugh or a pout. For others, emotions were subjective experiences. According to the American philosopher William James, emotions didn't *cause* physiological changes: they were the *experience* of these physiological changes. In other words, for him, emotions weren't a cause but an *effect*.

In the twentieth century, they were other things too, depending on how people defined them. In the first half of the century, when American psychologists largely ignored the mind (because the mind wasn't observable), they focused instead on behaviour. They studied fear as a behavioural response. In the second half of the century, when most psychologists were studying the mind again, they saw emotions as things that involved thought. For example, fear wasn't simply a behavioural response: it included an *awareness* of danger.

Some continued down the biological road. Like Darwin, they defined emotions as biological things, which could be seen in facial expressions. When people expressed, say, fear or anger, their expressions were remarkably similar. They were recognisable in different cultures and seemed to be universal. This suggested that emotions, such as fear and anger, were common to all humans and, therefore, the product of evolution. These 'basic emotions' were considered to be separate from the various kinds of actions and subjective experiences that might be associated with them.

However, others preferred a broader definition. Emotions, they felt, were defined by what the situation meant to the individual. They were *about* the situation, and what this meant depended on the context. For example, the same situation might provoke fear in some but not in others. Some social scientists pointed to ways in which emotions vary in different cultures. In doing so, they said little about biology. They focused on specific ways in which emotions were displayed, and how they were understood, within particular groups.

In other words, experts have come up with different ways to describe our feelings. Different emotional maps have been drawn, each providing a particular picture. They're not incompatible, but they focus on different aspects of the territory: for example, the role of biology, psychology or society in our emotional life. In the process, they made particular aspects of emotion relevant. When emotions were described as universal, they stressed the basic stuff that we have in common. When they claimed that emotions depended on the context, they stressed the various ways in which we understand and display our feelings.

As they drew particular maps, they also made different emotions obvious. Many argued that there were primary emotions but disagreed about what they were.[5] For some, love and shame were important. However, this was a minority view. Some lists of primary emotions included desire, guilt, interest and anticipation. However, most didn't. And what some regarded as key emotions (for example, surprise and interest) were, for others, cognitive states.[6] In other words, what some saw as obvious emotions were, to others, not really emotions. This was because they understood emotions in different ways. This led them to focus on different kinds of feelings.

This is what we do: we come up with ways to describe our feelings. We've done this in different ways. In the process, this has shaped our thoughts about which feelings matter.

The ways that we think about how we feel depend on the context in which we live.

Some emotions, depending on our time and place, may not be available. There may be culturally specific emotions, which are only experienced in certain societies. For example, 'amae' is a Japanese term that refers to a feeling of dependency and a desire to be loved, similar to a child's feelings towards its mother.[7] We don't have a word for it in English; though, as the last sentence shows, we can come up with some. However, if 'amae' is a specific emotion, then it doesn't seem to be widely available.

Historians have spoken of 'lost emotions', which we used to feel but no longer do. For example, in the medieval period, it was common (particularly for monks) to experience 'acedia'. This was described as a lack of caring, an inability to work or pray, which might lead to suicide. In that sense, it overlapped with what we now call 'depression', although it wasn't the same thing. It was part and parcel of a spiritual crisis and, in any case, the symptoms were different.[8] In short, we no longer experience 'acedia' as we used to. That particular feeling is no longer available.

Some emotions, depending on the context, may be more appealing than others. In recent years, one of the emotions that's become particularly appealing is 'wonder'.[9] However, this hasn't always been the case. There was a time when 'wonder' was associated with ignorance. It was seen as a lack of curiosity, which hampered enquiry by dulling the senses. Nevertheless, over time, 'wonder' came to be seen as more appealing.

Indeed, a few years ago, the philosopher Jesse Prinz suggested that wonder might be humanity's most important emotion. He was in good company. Richard Dawkins has described 'wonder' as the origin of scientific enquiry. Robert Fuller, a professor of Religious Studies, has claimed that 'wonder' is a principal source of spirituality. Long before them, Socrates said that 'wonder' was the beginning of philosophy and Descartes described it as the first of the passions. The origin of both science *and* religion? The beginning of both thinking *and* feeling? It's enough to make you wonder if they're all talking about the same thing.

Once again, it depends on what you mean. Socrates' 'wonder' was a sense of bewilderment followed by curiosity. Descartes' 'wonder' was a response to anything novel, which was removed by curiosity. We can 'wonder' in countless ways, which might provoke scientific enquiry or spirituality. We can 'wonder' about the origins of life, or at the beauty of a sunset, or if the train will arrive on time. We can experience 'wonder' in terms of 'astonishment', 'awe', 'dismay', 'admiration' or 'curiosity'. And, at times, we've tried to spot the

How we feel

differences. However, as always, these differences have been based on *particular* criteria.

For example, Thomas Brown distinguished between 'astonishment' and 'wonder' in terms of emotion and thought. For him, 'astonishment' was an emotion provoked by the unexpected, whereas 'wonder' involved 'contemplation'. His colleague, Charles Bell, distinguished between 'astonishment' and 'wonder' on the basis of facial expressions. For him, 'astonishment' could be seen in a blank expression, whereas 'wonder' could be seen in an eager face and a slightly open mouth. Others *equated* 'astonishment' with 'wonder', the main feature being 'an elation of tone'. But Darwin defined

According to Darwin, this is 'surprise', which can easily become 'astonishment', then 'stupefied amazement', which is 'closely akin to terror' (C. Darwin (1904). *The Expression of Emotion in Man and Animals*. London: John Murray, opposite p. 318).

'astonishment' as a form of surprise: one that was closer to fear. In other words, the difference between wonder and astonishment, if there was one, could be the difference between thinking and feeling, or a difference in facial expressions. And, if there wasn't one, then it could be a positive or a negative emotion.

As for the difference between 'wonder' and 'curiosity', these were classed as different kinds of emotions. Or else wonder was an emotion that was accompanied by curiosity (but curiosity was an 'instinct'). More recent psychologists have defined wonder as 'surprise'. But not if you mean in the sense of 'awe'. And, yes, some have even wondered if 'wonder' is really an emotion.[10]

Now, how does that make you feel?

Surprised?

Dismayed?

Or curious?

When it comes to how we feel, we really need to wonder – in the sense of being curious – what, precisely, we're talking about. After all, we seem to talk about our feelings more than ever. However, there's always a gap between how we feel and the words that we use to describe this. 'I feel fine.' What does that mean? Perhaps I'm very well, or just OK, or merely being polite, or hiding how I *really* feel. When we use emotion words, we may be telling a story to others. We may be telling ourselves a story. Either way, the story will depend on the emotional vocabulary that's available.

The words that we use define how we feel. However, we shouldn't mistake these words for the actual feelings that we have. The ways that we describe our feelings present a particular picture. They make some feelings more obvious or relevant. They make particular feelings available, or more appealing than others. Depending on the context, they suggest that some ways to feel are better than others.

This shapes our thoughts. We think about how we want to feel. We think about how to feel *that*. However, when we think in that way, we miss the bigger picture. The words that we use to describe our feelings, and the actual feelings that we have, are always part of a wider context.

What is love?
　　Love is blind.
　　Love is patient. Love is kind.
　　Love looks not with the eyes but with the mind.
　　But it's all so subjective and loosely defined.
　　Let's look at the facts and see what we find.
　　Once upon a time, a psychologist and a neuroscientist fell in love. The first lover said: 'I'm experiencing a feeling towards you that has three components which, in this particular combination, generate one of eight different kinds of love, and which is shaped by two factors: amount of love and balance of love.' And the second lover replied: 'Oh George, I've a surge of dopamine in my nucleus accumbens, my striatum and my ventral tegmental area.' And, according to findings based, respectively, on the Subjective Well-Being Scale and Functional Magnetic Resonance Imaging, they lived happily ever after.
　　Some emotions are better left to poets. The psychological facts about love are based on things that can be observed, such as responses to questionnaires or chemical changes in our individual brains when we lie in a brain scanner thinking about a loved one. The experience of love is more than that. If it wasn't, then we'd have little poetry, precious few songs, and remarkably empty lives.

There's a bigger picture to what we feel, what this means to us, and how this shapes our lives. In the real world, we experience countless feelings in response to countless events, which may lead us to think or act in countless ways. But how we understand these feelings can make a difference to how we feel, what we think, and how we act.

For example, when someone dies after a long and painful illness, we might feel grief or gratitude. We might feel guilty about feeling gratitude because the word suggests something else. Single words rarely capture what we feel. Fear can be of death, of boredom, of being noticed or of not being noticed, of being pregnant or of not being pregnant, of being alone or of making a commitment. The things that we feel, which shape what we do, may depend on what we think is too risky, or on what we think is too safe, but a surprising number will depend on what other people think and feel about us.

The feelings that we have, and how we display them, will depend on what seems normal at the time. Before the eighteenth century, for example, British grief was on limited display. At the time, infant mortality rates were such that the death of a child was normal. Later, during the Victorian period, funerals became extravagant affairs, with professional mourners, both adults and children, who expressed a solemn face for a fee. Tombstones were larger, houses were draped, and children were trained to express grief, sometimes with the help of special toys such as 'mourning dolls' (wax likenesses of the deceased) and 'death kits' (which included a doll and a miniature coffin). After the death toll of the Great War, however, displays of grief were considered less appealing. Emotional control was encouraged, and parents were advised to keep their children out of it. Excessive grief came to be seen as abnormal, and something which could be treated by bereavement counselling or as a new psychiatric disorder.[11]

The boundary between normal and abnormal feelings has always been fuzzy. As we increasingly talk about mental health, normal feelings are often described as if they're evidence of a disorder. This can make things worse for those who have more serious issues, and for those who only think that they do. If we feel 'depressed', then we might think this is a problem but, most of the time, it's not. It's perfectly normal to feel 'down' at times and, depending on the context, it would be stranger if we weren't. Clinical 'depression' is quite different. However, if we read about the symptoms, then we might identify with some of them, and think: that's how I feel.

That's because most of us feel some of these things, some of the time, depending on the context. Symptoms are guidelines, rules to be applied in a particular situation, and by experts. And these experts, often simply by talking to others, can change the way that they understand their feelings so that they think about them in different ways, act differently, and feel better. This will depend not simply on how people feel but also on what, precisely, the feelings are about, how long they have persisted, how they fit into the story of their lives so far, and the extent to which they cause distress and impair them in their current lives. In short, it will depend on the context in which these feelings happen.

Whatever the names that we use for the emotions, how we feel depends on the context. We can *be* guilty, according to the rules of others, and we can be embarrassed or shamed by others. Whether or not we *feel* guilty will depend on whether or not we agree with the rules. Whether we feel embarrassment or shame will depend on what we think (here and now) is normal or desirable. In the case of guilt, we can make amends, to the satisfaction of ourselves or others. We can apologise for an imperfect tweet and hope that this is sufficient. But we can't prevent the online shamers who condemn others from the unassailable position of righteous anonymity. A few years ago, when a woman made an ironic comment on Twitter – it was *obviously* ironic – she was bombarded with insults from strangers, received death threats and was sacked from her job.[12] Shame and guilt, whether or not we feel them, have long been forms of social control.

Emotions are both internal and external. They're understood through shared meanings, which are based on metaphors of external things. They're displayed on our faces and in our behaviour, and they're felt in response to events and people. They're used by some to limit our actions. We think of them as personal, but how we feel, what this means, and how this shapes our lives, is always part of a wider context.

So, we might do something radical: we might look beyond our personal feelings to notice the real world. It's easy today to feel more strongly about an imperfect tweet, or a disagreeable view, than about starving children or the exploitation of others, many of whom can't afford a device on which to tweet their personal grievances. Beyond our preoccupation with our own feelings, there are real-world problems which cause people to feel hungry and thirsty and in danger. That's the bigger picture. How do we feel about that? And, depending on how we feel about that, how might we wish to act? In the real world, how we feel, what we think, and what we do, are difficult to separate from each other.

Meanwhile, we've drawn a variety of boundaries – between thoughts and emotions, and between different emotions – using words with particular meanings. However, there are endless ways

How we feel

to describe our feelings and, if we wish, we can come up with more. If we want others to understand, then we need only point at something and explain what we mean. Take a look around. What do you see? Do you ever feel like a floor? Solid and dependable: you provide support for people, but then they just walk all over you? Do you ever feel like a window? Even if you don't open up, people can see right through you. If only you felt like a pair of curtains, then you could pull yourself together (smiley face).

Or, perhaps, you could look out of the window, at whatever is there, and think: I feel like *that*.

There are countless ways to describe our feelings. In different contexts, we've made particular feelings more obvious, or more available, or more appealing than others. This has shaped our thoughts about how we feel, and how we might want to feel.

Here and now, we want to feel happy. We think that this means getting what we want. If we don't feel happy, we think that it's a problem. If we don't have what we want, then we think about how we might get it. We think about how we feel and, in turn, this shapes our thoughts. Our feelings and thoughts are connected.

It's been more than two centuries since Thomas Brown drew a boundary between emotions and thoughts. For much of that time, we've thought of them as distinct and opposing entities. We've thought that emotions cloud our reason. In the world of critical thinking, they've been seen as another source of error: for example, we can be persuaded by appeals to emotion, which lead us to think in irrational ways.

Reason, however, is a means to an end. It doesn't tell us what the end should be. That depends on what we want. What we want will depend, of course, on what we feel is desirable. This is always part of a wider context. If we want to feel happy – or to get what we want – then we can use reason. Before we do that, however, we really need to think about what we want. After all, what we want – like what we notice, how we interpret it, what we believe, what we take for granted, what we find persuasive, and how we feel – shapes our thoughts.

As I stand here, at the entrance of Old College, I still feel like George Square. Before I head back, however, there's one more curious thing that I want to point out.

8

What we want

I'm heading east from Old College, crossing South Bridge, and walking down Infirmary Street.

At the end of Infirmary Street is the building that was once the Royal High School. In 1778, a young Walter Scott became a pupil here. Many years later, Scott would be one of the most influential men of his age. However, by his own admission, he wasn't the best of pupils: 'I glanced,' he recalled, 'like a meteor from one end of the class to the other.'[1] Scott's later success in life was, according to one biographer, an illustration of the 'power of perseverance'.[2]

When Scott was here, this street was called Jamaica Street, but they changed the name. For many years, the Royal Infirmary was here. When Charles Darwin was studying medicine, he attended two operations here, but 'rushed away before they were completed … this being long before the blessed days of chloroform'.[3] His medical studies didn't last. A few years later, however, another medical student would show more perseverance. In 1829, a young man called Samuel Smiles finished his medical training here.[4]

Thirty years later, like Darwin, Samuel Smiles became famous. And, like him, it wasn't for medicine. Like Darwin, Smiles became famous for a book that he published in 1859. Darwin's *On the Origin of Species* would be one of the most influential books of the century. However, over the course of the century, Smiles' book would sell more than five times as many copies. The reason for its remarkable popularity was that it taught the public how to improve their lives. The book was called *Self-Help*. It was the original self-help book.

The book has a curious history. It's a reminder that, whatever you want, you need to think about the bigger picture. So, before I head back from the old Royal High School to George Square, there's a lesson to be learned.

Whatever you want, it shapes your thoughts. What you notice, and how you interpret it, depends on what you find appealing. You tend to believe what you want to believe. You also think explicitly about what you want, and about how to get it. This determines the questions that you ask and the answers that you seek.

However, the things that you want are shaped by others. They make some things obvious, and relevant, to you. They make them available, and appealing, to you.

The lesson – and it's a radical one – is this: there's a bigger picture … it's not all about *you*.

Self-Help was a themed collection of true stories of success. It was inspired by the lives of Smiles' heroes. It was the first of the countless bestselling self-help books that have continued to appear ever since. However, its lessons were radically different.

Smiles didn't pretend that success was easy because, as any true success story shows, and as any truly successful person knows, success is hard. Smiles' advice wasn't based on simple rules. It was based on how individuals had persevered in difficult circumstances. For him, success was not only hard, but also had little to do with fame or fortune. It was about building character, gaining self-respect, being independent and recognising the worth of others.

In the decades after the success of *Self-Help*, a string of new self-help books appeared. They offered a remarkable range of ever-so-simple secrets about how to succeed. Self-improvers were told how to become more intelligent, how to gain a better memory, and how to *Think and Grow Rich*. Or, for those who found thinking too strenuous, how to *Grow Rich While You Sleep*. They were told *How to Win Friends and Influence People* and how to exploit *The Power of Positive Thinking* for a better, happier and more satisfying life. Combinations of New Age thought, pop psychology and business tips were produced for a growing population who increasingly noticed – because it was increasingly being brought to their attention – that their lives weren't good enough.

Nevertheless, throughout all of this, Smiles' original *Self-Help* book continued to appear. With countless new editions, in dozens of languages, it continued to espouse its original message. Until 1986.

That was when yet another edition of *Self-Help* appeared. But this was the edition for the Thatcher generation. It had an introduction by Sir Keith Joseph, Thatcher's intellectual guru and Secretary of State for Education. According to Sir Keith, *Self-Help* was 'a book for *our* times' (original italics). It expressed the spirit of the Thatcher period.[5]

However, for anyone familiar with the original edition of *Self-Help*, or any of the countless editions since, the Thatcherite edition looked strangely different. It wasn't obvious. If you only saw the 1986 edition, then you wouldn't know what you were missing. You wouldn't notice that this was a particular picture.

For one thing, it was smaller than the earlier editions. It was significantly shorter because it was abridged. It was abridged by a man who, as it happens, later received an OBE from Thatcher. The Thatcherite edition of *Self-Help* had been downsized. One fifth of the original book had been deleted. In the process, it had become a book that expressed the spirit of Thatcherism.

Now, a curious person might wonder what, precisely, had been deleted. After all, if one wishes to make cuts of 20 per cent, then such drastic reductions shouldn't be random. The bits to be cut should be cut for a reason. And, if somebody were curious, then they might take the time to compare the original *Self-Help* with the Thatcherite edition.[6]

So that they could spot the differences.

To see what, precisely, was excluded.

If only out of curiosity.

When you compare the two editions, you notice that some curious things are missing.

For example, Thatcher was a grocer's daughter. This was well known because she often used to point it out. And, as it happens, the original edition of *Self-Help* makes some remarks about grocers. It refers to one as 'an unhappy youth who committed suicide a few years since because he had been "born to be a man and condemned to be a grocer"'.[7] It wasn't that Smiles had a problem with the profession. For him, it was 'not the calling that degrades the man, but the man that degrades the calling'.[8] However, when seeking an example of a man who was 'dreadfully condescending, and cannot avoid seizing on every opportunity to make his greatness felt', the example that he chose was a grocer.[9] But the readers of

What we want

the Thatcherite edition would never know. These comments about members of the profession of Thatcher's father were deleted.

Of course, it might just be a coincidence, but other professions got a different treatment. In 1986, Thatcher was probably best known as the woman who defeated the miners. She'd abridged the mining industry with an enthusiasm that led to national strikes and violent clashes, defiance followed by defeat, and a further increase in unemployment. Whatever one made of the miners' strike, Thatcher and the miners were not on good terms. And, perhaps it's mere coincidence again but, in the original edition of *Self-Help*, there's a single sentence at the end of a paragraph on page 206. However, it was deleted from the 1986 edition. A single sentence, that's all, and it's hard to imagine why it would be deleted. It refers to miners. It refers to them as 'kind'.

> works, to every part of which he had access; and he seized the opportunity thus afforded him of storing his mind with observations, and mastering, as he thought, the mechanism of iron splitting. After a continued stay for this purpose, he suddenly disappeared from amongst his kind friends the miners—no one knew whither.
> Returned to England, he communicated the results of his voyage to Mr. Knight and another person at Stourbridge,

> Dannemora mines, near Uppsala. He was received into the works, to every part of which he had access; and he seized the opportunity thus afforded him of storing his mind with observations, and mastering, as he thought, the mechanism of iron splitting.
> Returned to England, he communicated the results of his voyage to Mr Knight and another person at Stourbridge, who had sufficient

Above: from page 206 of the 1886 edition. Below: the same passage from the (abridged) 1986 edition, which deleted the reference to 'his kind friends the miners'.

Radical Thinking

For the most part, however, Smiles' original *Self-Help* tells the lives of various leaders of industry. These include John Heathcoat, inventor of the bobbin net, a complex machine for making lace-like material. It is, like so many of the mini-biographies, a tale of perseverance in the face of seemingly insurmountable obstacles. In the Thatcherite edition of *Self-Help*, we're told of Heathcoat's final success. We're not told of the episode when rioters, whose jobs were threatened by his new machines, burned down his factory. We're not told that ten of the rioters were subsequently caught and eight of them were executed. And we're not told that, despite his personal hardships and financial loss at the hands of rioters, Heathcoat became the most benevolent of employers, who 'carefully provided for their comfort and improvement'. He didn't 'close his heart against the claims of the poor and struggling, who were always sure of his sympathy and help'.[10]

Other acts of benevolent employers towards the less fortunate also failed to make it into the Thatcherite edition. For example, Smiles told of how the first Sir Robert Peel (father of the future Tory prime minister), who made his fortune in cotton printing, promoted 'the well-being and comfort of [his] workpeople, for whom [he] contrived to provide remunerative employment even in the least prosperous times'.[11] But this was deleted.

References to individual greed were also removed. Smiles wrote that greed 'defiles'.[12] He compared the 'love of wealth' to the foolish greed of a monkey.[13] He told his readers about a man who worked hard to become rich, but since he didn't share his wealth, his life was 'sordid' and he 'died an inveterate miser'. 'With a nobler spirit,' Smiles declared, 'the same determination might have enabled such a man to be a benefactor to others as well as himself.'[14] However, that was deleted.

The most obvious theme of the bits that were deleted from the Thatcherite edition is this: the theme of helping others. Their names may no longer be remembered, but their actions were included by Smiles for a reason. He told his readers of how Jacques Callot was helped by Gypsies, of the generosity of Francis Chantrey, and of the kindness of neighbours to John Flaxman.[15] He told them about John Howard helping prisoners, about Thomas Wright helping ex-convicts, about Ambroise Paré helping soldiers, about Joseph Hume helping poor relations, about David Barclay helping the poor of Walthamstow, about Francis Xavier helping the poor of Goa, about John Pounds helping the poor of Portsmouth, and about Jonas Hanway helping the poor of Montreal, London and Barbados.[16] But all of this was deleted.

And yet, perhaps, the most interesting deletion is that of Adam Smith. He appears in the earlier editions, but he doesn't appear in the 1986 edition. This is odd, because Adam Smith is often seen as the founder of free-market economics. His most famous book, *The Wealth of Nations*, proposed a theory of self-interest that was espoused with enthusiasm by Thatcher, Ronald Reagan and right-wing economists of that time. His name was adopted by the free-market think tank, the Adam Smith Institute, founded shortly after Thatcher became Conservative leader, and which provided the intellectual basis for various Thatcherite policies. So, you have to wonder why on earth would Adam Smith be deleted from a book that, according to Thatcher's intellectual guru, expresses the spirit of Thatcherism?

Perhaps because no person is just one thing. Before Adam Smith became the hero of the free market, he was a moral philosopher at the University of Glasgow. He formed a theory of human morality based on the idea of sympathy. For Smith, we're driven not only by

Radical Thinking

self-interest but also by sympathy. The latter is a universal human feeling towards others that inclines us to want to help them regardless of any material reward. It's the Adam Smith of sympathy, rather than of self-interest, who appears in the original *Self-Help*: as an example of a 'labourer for the public good … uncheered by the prospect of immediate recompense or result'.[17] But that was deleted.

Having removed remarks about kind miners, benevolent employers, criticisms of greed, and praise for those who helped the poor, the 1986 edition of *Self-Help* deleted the hero of the free market for showing his sympathetic side. The cuts were made, the fat was trimmed, and the waste was tossed away. *Self-Help* was now leaner and meaner. In short, it was more selfish.

It's a reflection of the world of self-help more generally. The self-help books of the last generation have been more self-centred than ever before. Smiles had shown how self-improvement came from application and perseverance, yet today's bestselling self-help books offer easy solutions that are supposed to change our lives by following a few simple rules. Smiles wanted us to build character and self-respect, but we're now offered self-obsession dressed up as spirituality. Is this really what you want?

If so, and you wish to save yourself a few pounds, here are the basic secrets of success:

> Think about what you want a lot.
> Imagine getting it.
> Try to get it.
> Act nice to people (so they help you get it).
> Don't give up (or you might not get it).
> Love yourself (in case you don't get it).

What we want

The problem is that, while most of these 'secrets' are basic common sense, they're not common practice. The real secret isn't the knowledge of some rules but the translation of these rules into practice, which takes actual hard work and perseverance in the face of whatever might arise. And, of course, however hard you try, it may not work out. It's a process, not an outcome. What isn't common knowledge is that this was said in the original self-help book.

But the book was also about helping *other people*. Then it was transformed into something else, and how that was done may be the only genuine secret relating to self-help. As these bits about helping others were deleted, it became increasingly about *you*.

When you think about what *you* want, of course, you think about what you're missing. As you do, you miss the bigger picture: it's not all about *you*.

Once upon a time, just round the corner from here, a performer was doing a show at the Edinburgh Festival. She needed some people to hand out promotional flyers to advertise her show. So, one day, at the break of dawn, she went out to hire some workers.

She found some people doing nothing and told them: if you hand out these flyers for the day, then I shall pay you a pound. And they agreed. This was the 1980s. Jobs were in short supply, and they needed the money. So, they were grateful for the work.

And then, about noon, she went out again and saw more people doing nothing, and she told them: if you hand out these flyers for the rest of the day, then I shall pay you. And they agreed, because they also needed the money.

And then, a few hours later, she went out again and saw more people doing nothing, and she told them: if you hand out these flyers for the rest

Radical Thinking

of the day, then I shall pay you. And they also agreed, because they needed the money.

At the end of the day, the people lined up to get paid. Those who had been working since dawn were paid a pound. As they had been promised. However, those who had been working since noon, and those who had been working for only a few hours, were also paid a pound.

The people who had been working since dawn were now peeved. They didn't think that this was right. 'We've been working all day,' they complained, 'yet we've been paid no more than those who worked far fewer hours.'

And the performer told them: 'I promised you a pound and I gave you a pound, and what I pay the others is none of your concern.'

And the people who had been working since dawn walked away, feeling cheated, and decided to form a union.

The story isn't true, as far as I know, though nothing is certain and anything is possible. But I've no evidence that it really happened. As some of you might have spotted, it's based on the parable of the vineyard owner.[18] By Jesus. In other words, it's as true as the original. The moral of the original parable is that, regardless of how long you've been faithful, you can still receive your heavenly reward. However, there's a real-world lesson here.

The all-day workers were initially happy. They had no work and were given work. However, they were unhappy later because, despite getting what they were promised, others got a better deal.

The lesson of the parable is this: what we want is shaped by other people. They show us what the options are.

What do you want?

It depends on the options.

After all, we all want stuff. We *need* food, clothing and shelter. We *want* particular kinds of food, particular kinds of clothes, and a particular kind of home, and then we want to fill that home with more stuff that we don't really need. These wants are in our heads, but they didn't start there. Nobody is born with the desire to have a McDonald's burger, or a pair of Nike trainers, or a flat-screen television. These wants aren't natural.

Some things are natural. For example, hair. Animals have hair and humans have hair. But *we* don't want the hair that we have. We're told that we have too much hair, or too little, or that it's in the wrong places. We're told that our hair shouldn't be grey, or dry, or brittle: it should be shiny and bouncy. When we buy into this, we buy the merchandise: razors, trimmers, hair-removal cream, hair dye or a special shampoo and conditioner, as used by professionals, because we're worth it. We're shown images of others who seem happy because their hair is shiny and bouncy.

This isn't entirely new, but how it happens has changed. In the nineteenth century, what was going on was obvious because advertising was based on product information. It stressed the product's practical value. At the end of the nineteenth century, most advertising experts still thought that the purpose of the advertisement was to inform the potential buyer.[19] By the twentieth century, however, mass production had led to supply exceeding demand. Producers, therefore, had to create demand for things that people didn't need. They had to find a way to get us to buy more of this and that. And, as producers competed with each other, they tried to encourage us to buy their own brand of this or that.

For over a century, we've been told what to want. None of this was obvious. They had to appeal to us. They had to tell us that these things, which we didn't need, were nevertheless relevant to us. They did this by presenting a particular picture: if you buy this, then you'll feel better. We naturally wanted to feel happy and healthy, so products were marketed to appeal to this desire.

We were told about products that we didn't have, and we were shown other people who had them. And *they* certainly appeared to be happy and healthy. In one old advert, a family of three are in beachwear. They're slim and healthy and smiling broadly ('They're happy because they eat lard'). In another old advert, a happy couple struggle to conceal their embarrassment as they model inflatable pants ('Look better – feel better' and 'slenderize exactly where you want' with "Wonder Sauna Hot Pants" – reduces waist, tummy, hips, and thighs').

Or reduce weight by eating less. How? For example, by smoking more. In another old advert, a young athlete leaps a hurdle as his obese shadow lurks behind him ('When tempted to over-indulge, reach for a Lucky [Strike] instead'). It was important, of course, to smoke the healthiest cigarettes. In another ad, a man in a white coat holds a cigarette, below the caption: 'Most Doctors Smoke Camels'. By making particular facts relevant, anything could be presented as a way to become healthier.

Advertisers didn't simply tap into things that people already wanted. They also convinced us to want new things by making a problem relevant and then selling us the solution. Psychologists called this the creation of 'wants and solutions'.[20] Sometimes the problem had to be pointed out, however, because it was far from obvious. For example, until the 1920s, halitosis wasn't well known. However, Listerine had mouthwash to sell, so they made the problem obvious. They showed us that others had it and, therefore, that we might have it too.

Their adverts encouraged paranoia about having bad breath ('The whispers he never heard ... His wife ought to tell him. Do they say it of you? – probably'). They explained that there was no way of knowing ('Even your best friend won't tell you'). But they pointed out that others knew ('They talk about you behind your back. And rightly so – halitosis is inexcusable'). They pointed out that this was unappealing ('Halitosis makes you unpopular').

It affected salesmen ('Keep your salesman out of my office!'). Or those trying to get a new job ('So <u>that's</u> why he didn't get the job!'). And, if you had a job, then you might lose it ('Halitosis may get you discharged'). It affected families ('Are you unpopular with your own children?'). Though, unlike your friends, your children *will* tell you ('If you want the truth – go to a child'). After all, they were getting into fights at school (because 'Jimmy's dad has halitosis').

However, they focused particularly on women ('No male for the girl who has bad breath'). You'll not get a boyfriend ('He's not going to call!'). Or if you do, then it won't last ('You can lose him in a minute!'). And you'll not know the reason ('His letter didn't explain why'). Some messages were repeated, over and over again, with tiny variations in punctuation ('Often a bridesmaid ... never a bride!', 'Often a bridesmaid ... Never a bride!', 'Often a bridesmaid but never a bride', 'Often a bridesmaid, but never a bride!'). However, they also provided a solution: with the wonders of Listerine, romance would return ('Back in his heart ... Again!') and marriage would follow ('as he carried her across the threshold ... a girl with breath as sweet as the blossoms in her bridal bouquet').

They tapped into stereotypes. They reflected what they thought, in that time and place, was normal. However, if an alternative view became popular, then they could appeal to a new customer base.

Radical Thinking

When women's rights became increasingly relevant, one of the ways that feminists challenged gender stereotypes was by smoking in public (something that wasn't considered ladylike and, in some places, was then illegal). Edward Bernays, the public relations guru, saw a chance to profit from this. In 1929, he organised a march in New York, one of the places where women weren't allowed to smoke in public. He hired young women to march in the Easter Parade while smoking Lucky Strike cigarettes. Or, as he called them, their 'Torches of Freedom'. Adverts celebrated this act of emancipation ('An ancient prejudice has been removed'). Meanwhile, women continued to be targeted along more traditional lines ('To keep a slender figure, reach for a Lucky').

These adverts worked by appealing to the wants of potential customers in a particular context. That's why, here and now, they seem extraordinary. The context has changed. But so have the adverts. They still do the same thing as they did before, but it's not so obvious because they tap into what we currently want.

We continue to want to be happy and healthy, look good and feel free, but in different ways now. We still want stuff that we think will make us feel better, but we often forget about the bigger picture. Depending on the context, we want the basics of food and water, comfort and safety. We want, if we can have them, human relationships, a sense of belonging, and a feeling of worth. And, when everything else has been covered, we want to reach our full potential, whatever that might mean. But whatever our ongoing wants might be, the specific solutions available to us depend on what can be seen in the shop window.

We continue to be customers whose individual needs might be satisfied by available products. A new self-help book. Or a better conditioner. Or the latest version of the thing that we have. A new you. Or shinier hair. Or the new shiny thing. Is there anything more? There's plenty more. There are endless variations on display in the window. And one of them is just right for *you*.

There is, however, a bigger picture. We want things as individuals, as groups, and as a species: a new car to drive, our economy to thrive, and a planet on which we can survive. But these different wants are often at odds with each other. At that point, we need to think about priorities. It has become increasingly normal to think about individual priorities. However, no matter how individual you are, if you merely want to survive, then you'll need a planet that hasn't been destroyed by others. In modern society, if you want the basics, then you'll need to get them from others. If you want relationships, a sense of belonging and a feeling of worth, then you can't do this by yourself. And, if you simply want to be happy, then you might think about helping others. After all, according to numerous psychological studies, the overall finding is this: helping others leads to greater happiness.[21]

Samuel Smiles would have agreed. When *Self-Help* became a bestseller, he felt, in hindsight, that the title was unfortunate. This 'has led some, who have judged it merely by the title, to suppose that it consists of a eulogy of selfishness – the very opposite of what it really is'. So, he made it clear: 'the duty of helping one's self in the highest sense involves the helping of one's neighbours.'[22]

Whatever you want, one way or another, it will depend on other people. They show you what's available. They make particular things appealing. They display a limited of number of things and present them in a particular way. They provide you with a menu of options, from which you're free to choose. Naturally, you prefer some things to others. In the process, this shapes your thoughts.

Beyond the shop window, there's what you're missing. It's not out there in the world that you see. It's in the ways that you see the world: in the questions that you ask and the answers that you seek.

What do *you* want?

What do *we* want?

The answers to these are often very different.

When we look at the world from an individual perspective, of course, it's obvious to think about personal wants. And there are individual solutions available. For example, if *you* just want to feel happy, then there's a secret. And it's remarkably simple: *lower your expectations*.

This appears to have been confirmed by neuroscience. According to recent findings, a personal feeling of 'momentary happiness' depends not on things going well but on things going better than expected.[23] And, if happiness is a fleeting personal feeling, then that makes complete sense.

However, beyond your fleeting personal feelings, there's what you want to do in life. Whatever it is, if you want to succeed, then it won't be so easy. Smiles' heroes didn't lower their expectations. When things didn't go as expected, they persevered. As Smiles put it – and he said this in reference to Walter Scott – they succeeded through the 'power of perseverance'.

Whatever you want to achieve, it will take perseverance. However, it will also depend on others. They'll provide you with options and suggest solutions. They'll offer feedback and give guidance to you. And, if you want a greater sense of satisfaction, then you might want to do something for others. Whatever route you take, you'll not be taking it alone. Along the way, of course, your individual brain will have countless fleeting feelings. However, as we'll shortly see, your individual brain is only part of the picture.

For the moment, however, the lesson is over.

* * *

When the young Walter Scott had finished his lessons, he walked back from the old Royal High School to his home on George Square. I'm going to do the same.

On the way back, he passed the university, which he would later attend. At the time, the buildings were in a ruinous condition. A few years later, the building of the 'New College' would begin. As it was being completed, Thomas Brown would invent the category of 'the emotions'. Later still, Professor Bennett and Professor Gregory would argue about the power of mesmerism to influence people. At the time, of course, young Walter hadn't heard of 'the emotions' or of the power of mesmerism. It's a reminder that how we understand our feelings, and the ways that we can be persuaded, depends on the context.

As he walked home, young Walter may have known that, half a mile away, an impressive monument had just been built above the grave of David Hume. But he couldn't have known that, just across the road from the Hume monument – the road now known as Waterloo Place – they would erect a monument to Nelson. Hume, the sceptic who questioned the most obvious things, though he had his own limits. The Nelson Monument, a giant telescope that can't see beyond its own foundations. It's a reminder that our thoughts are limited by the things that we take for granted, and by our current points of view.

Radical Thinking

As he walked back to George Square – the same as I'm doing now – young Walter would have seen things differently. He would have walked up Jamaica Street. This is now Infirmary Street. Same street, different name. He would have turned south on Potterrow. Potterrow has changed significantly. Same name, different street. At the time, a wall divided Jamaica Street from Nicolson Street. Today, there are bridges that connect Nicolson Street all the way to New Town. It's a reminder that we give particular names to things, and we draw particular boundaries – however, these aren't fixed.

When young Walter was walking home, a map of here looked very different from a current map. If I compare the maps, then I can spot the differences. However, I can't see young Walter's world with my own eyes. I've no access to the actual territory. When I interpret his world, as I'm doing now, I need to rely on the map. I rely on whatever descriptions are available: they include some things and leave out others. It's a reminder of how we interpret the world: we create different maps of the territory. And, beyond our own experience, we need to rely on the descriptions of others, who present a particular picture.

As he walked back to George Square, the second edition of *Encyclopaedia Britannica* was still being completed, but he wouldn't have passed the printing shop on Nicolson Street where it first appeared. It's a reminder that our view of the world is always a limited picture. When he arrived home at 25 George Square, he couldn't have known that, a century later, Arthur Conan Doyle would be living at number 23. For him, that knowledge wasn't available. To me, however, this is obvious. I made it relevant in Chapter 1, when I pointed out that there are exactly four steps outside number 23. I now see that, outside number 25, there are only three steps. I hadn't noticed that before. It's a reminder of how little we notice.

The route that young Walter took, though it ended up in the same position, wasn't the same as mine. Whatever the outcome, however, we can still think about the process. Our thoughts are shaped by what we notice, by how we interpret what we see and hear, by our points of view and what we take for granted, by what we find persuasive, how we feel and what we want.

Nevertheless, if we're curious, we can look beyond our own limited observations and interpretations, our own beliefs and assumptions, our own feelings and desires. Whatever might be in our individual brains, we can see where we are within the bigger picture.

To do that, however, we need to think more critically about our own position, and about what others tell us. So, it's now time to move on to the second part of the book.

PART 2

Thinking in a Radical Way

9

Where are we?

First, we need to think about our own position.

I'm back in the office. I'm looking out of the window. I'm located in a small space, staring out at the rest of the world. You're somewhere else, in a space of some kind – at home, perhaps, or on a bus, or a train, or a plane, or in an airport lounge – which has a window with a different view. We appear to be disconnected.

And yet, here and now, we're connected. We're here: at the beginning of Chapter 9, at the start of the second part of the book. I'm writing this. You're reading this. I'm putting down these thoughts, which are in my head, and now these same thoughts are in your head. There are connections that we can't see, which bind us, wherever we happen to be. It's important to remember these connections, because – and I'm telling you this because we're in this together – some people have a very limited view of you.

It began when, a few decades ago, advances in neuroscience led to an astonishing claim: 'You are your brain.'[1] Since then, the claim has been repeated, over and over again: 'You are your brain,' 'You are your brain.'[2] According to various reports, whatever you think – no matter what you think – it's all in your brain. Your

Radical Thinking

political views and religious beliefs are the product of your brain chemistry.[3] Your moral compass is in your brain (but so, alas, is your capacity for evil).[4] You're hard-wired to be racist, to believe in God, to be addicted to porn, and to accept health advice from celebrities.[5] It seems that no matter who you are, or what you think, there's no escape: You are your brain. It really is an astonishing claim.

However, it's also a trap. It imprisons you in a small space, staring out at the rest of the world while feeling disconnected from it. If you want to escape, then there's an alternative perspective: you're *not* your brain.[6] You're a person with a body. Your brain is part of your body. And, yes, it's a remarkable part. Nevertheless, it has its limits. It can't walk or talk. It can't laugh or cry. It can't eat or drink. Or go to the toilet. It can't kiss, or have sex, or have children, or raise them. There are all sorts of things that *you* can do, but your brain can't do, because you're *not* your brain.

Your brain, of course, is the centre of your thinking. However, it's not the whole of your thinking. From the moment you're born, you're constantly interacting with the world and with other people. In the process, you work out what to think about politics, religion or anything else. Naturally, what you think depends on connections in your brain. However, it also depends on other connections: the ones between our brains. These connections are in what we say and do. They're in the ways that we interact with the world outside, and with each other. Without these connections, we would not, and could not, think the way that we do.

Whatever is currently in your brain, you can look farther: to how it got there. If you remember the things that shape your thoughts, which we've been discussing so far, then you can see where you are within the bigger picture.

And, since we're currently connected – we're here together in Chapter 9, at the beginning of the second part of the book – we can use this as a reminder of how we got here. After we've done this, we'll be in a better position to see where we're going.

As we discussed in the first two chapters, whatever you think, or think about, depends on what you notice. You notice what's obvious and whatever is available. You're attracted to what's appealing and what seems relevant to you. You then need to *interpret* what you notice. As we discussed in Chapter 3, you understand everything through the medium of language: using words that have particular meanings, and categories that draw particular boundaries. This happens inside your brain.

Nevertheless, your thoughts are shaped by things outside your brain. They're *about* the things that you notice: the things that you see, or hear, or read about. You then need to interpret these in a language that was taught to you by others. In a language that was *created* by others. They came up with words and agreed on what they meant. They came up with categories by drawing particular boundaries between this and that. The language through which you understand everything evolved over time, and it continues to evolve, because it's the product of human interaction. Without it, the thoughts inside your brain – about politics, religion or anything else – would be astonishingly limited.

What you believe depends on how you interpret what you notice. As we discussed in Chapter 4, you can always interpret the facts so that they fit with your existing beliefs. This will depend on what seems normal, ordinary or natural to you. And this happens inside your brain. However, what your beliefs *might be* depends on the

Radical Thinking

options that are out there. You hear people express views, or read about them, and *then* decide if you agree. You choose your beliefs from a long menu that's already out there in the world. This menu is shaped by what, in a particular context, is considered normal. As we discussed in Chapter 5, what you believe depends on what you take for granted. This is shaped by local customs and habits. And, as we discussed in Chapter 6, it depends on what you find convincing. This is shaped by other people, who do their best to persuade you. But whatever beliefs you choose from the menu – about politics, religion or anything else – they began outside your head.

Your feelings are responses to external events, which make you feel … what? As we discussed in Chapter 7, you understand how *you* feel in a language that others created. The words through which you understand your feelings are based on metaphors of external things. And these feelings are reactions to things out there. Typically, the actions of others. They make you feel happy or sad, or offended, depending on what they say or do. You then display this in your behaviour to others. Meanwhile, depending on the time and place in which you live, you're guided by others to feel this not that, and to act accordingly.

As we discussed in Chapter 8, your desires are shaped by other people. The things that you want are *made* desirable by parents and teachers, politicians and priests, and by people who want to sell you things. Nobody is hard-wired to want a respectable career, or to pass an exam, or to vote for lower taxes, or to pray for forgiveness from an invisible power. Nobody is hard-wired to want bouncy hair. Whatever you think, or think about – whatever you believe, or feel, or want – it's shaped by other people.

Now we're here in Chapter 9, remembering how we got here. These memories are in your brain. But your memories aren't just in your brain. You can remember things by writing a shopping list, by posting a Post-it, or by setting an alarm clock. You can recall the past by buying souvenirs. You can record memories in a diary, or in photographs that you can show to others (indeed, the point of photographs now seems to be *merely* to show to others). You can see reminders, on the road and in the toilet, to wear your seatbelt and to wash your hands.

Whatever you think, it's not just your brain. That's why you're thinking this, right now, instead of something else. We put our thoughts out there, and the things that we think are responses to what others say and do. Together, we work out what to think, how to feel, and who we are.

Now, where was I?

I was looking out of the window from a small space, feeling disconnected from the outside world. I was thinking that I'm here, alone, and that my view is limited. And my view *is* limited. However, it's not *that* limited. If I was simply my brain, then I'd be trapped here. But I'm not my brain. I'm a person with a body, who can walk and talk. I can interact with the world and others. I can walk up a hill and see farther. I can talk to others and hear alternative views. This will shape how I think about the world of people and things, and about my place within it. I don't need to be limited by the window through which I currently look.

So, I'm going outside.

To the east, I can see the Radical Road. If I walked that road, then I'd see farther and would encounter different views. Alternative perspectives are essential. They make other things obvious and

Radical Thinking

available. They find other things appealing and relevant. They help us to see the assumptions that we make – about what we mean by the names and categories that we use, about the boundaries that we draw between this and that, or between them and us – which define every person and thing that we think about. They provide us with more than one map of the territory, each one presenting a particular picture. Each of them may seem convincing because, whatever the facts, they're presented in a way that's designed to persuade us. However, if we compare them and spot the differences, then we can make better sense of the territory.

It may seem that you're in a small space, looking out at a separate world. The window through which you look may be narrow. But, if you're curious, then you can see that you're a part of something larger. Your thoughts are not entirely yours. The things that you think, or feel, or want, are shaped by the world in which you live. It's not all about you. However, if you see the bigger picture, then you can discover your place within it. In other words, it's up to you.

But this will require some critical thinking.

This is where we began, at the start of the book and, having walked around the square, we've now returned to where we started. In the beginning, I mentioned that 'critical thinking' is typically discussed in terms of the rules of logic and science: in particular, the logical fallacies and cognitive biases that lead to erroneous outcomes. However, along the way, we've seen that – in terms of the process – there are many other things that shape our thoughts.

So, we're now in a position to think about critical thinking in a more radical way.

It's time to think about where we're going.

What, precisely, is 'critical thinking'? After all, everyone thinks that 'critical thinking' is a good thing. Everyone. Even fundamentalists.

Ken Ham, the creationist who built a Creation Museum in Kentucky – it displays dinosaurs in the Garden of Eden – believes that the Book of Genesis is historically accurate. He believes that God created the universe around 6,000 years ago – because the Bible tells him so. He refuses to believe in any facts that contradict this belief. Yet Ham is a fan of 'critical thinking'. For him, and other fundamentalists, 'critical thinking' is needed to question evolutionary theory and the facts on which it's based.[7]

This is the first problem with 'critical thinking': when people talk about it, they're talking about different things. Even the experts can't agree on what 'critical thinking' is. It's been defined as an individual trait, as an attitude, as a performance, as an ability, and as a combination of specific skills. For some, 'critical thinking' is a matter of logic. For others, it's the application of scientific methods. For others still, it's a form of reflective thinking that questions assumptions, including the ones on which science is based.[8] 'Critical thinking' means different things to different people.

So, to think in a 'critical' way, you need to begin by asking: what does that *mean*?

This brings us to the second problem of 'critical thinking': how do you do it? Most experts point out that 'critical thinking' should be based on the methods of logic and science. And, compared to the fundamentalists, that's a better basis on which to think. However, this has its limits. The methods of logic and science are fine things to learn. However, in the real world, knowledge is messier than in the classroom and the laboratory. People play by different rules, and base

Radical Thinking

their conclusions on different criteria. Nevertheless, that needn't be a problem: thinking critically is a process, not an outcome. Whatever your conclusion – whether you think *this* or *that* – it's not about where you end up: it's about how you get there.

So, to think in a critical way, we need to ask: what's the *basis* of this or that?

This brings us to the third problem: what's the purpose of 'critical thinking'. Depending on what you think it is, 'critical thinking' is what you use to identify a dodgy argument, to reduce bias, to make better decisions, to solve problems, to find more creative solutions and to avoid coming to the wrong conclusions. No wonder that everyone, even fundamentalists, thinks that this is a good thing. They simply disagree about what counts as a dodgy argument, a biased view, a better decision, a good solution or a correct conclusion.

So, to think in a critical way, we need to ask: what's the *purpose*?

As some of the experts have pointed out, whatever 'critical thinking' is, it's always thinking *about something*.[9] So, let me be more specific: we're going to think about thinking critically, but not in the sense of problem-solving, decision-making or creative thinking. We're going to think about knowledge claims. The things that we read or hear or say, which state that 'this' or 'that' is the case. In short, the things that we think.

To think critically about knowledge claims, we need to go beyond the abstract rules of logic and science, the lists of fallacies and biases to which we're prone, and the comforting myth that, if we know what not to do, then we'll no longer do it. We need to think about how we can actually think 'critically' in the real world. We'll do this by asking some questions.

Whatever the claim might be – about politics, religion or anything else – we need to consider three questions. First, when someone makes a claim, what do they really *mean*? Second, what's the *basis* of that claim? Third, what is its *purpose*? If we do that, then we can make sense of any claim that we encounter.

Nevertheless, we're going to begin with the obvious ways of thinking about critical thinking: logic and science. We're going to do that because they're remarkably useful. We just need to remember their limits.

And, of course, we can do that from here.

10

The limits of logic

George Square is in Edinburgh.
I'm in George Square.
Therefore: I'm in Edinburgh.

That seems logical. If the first two statements are true, then the conclusion must be true.

And, as it happens, the first two statements are true. So, logically speaking (i.e. based on logical deduction), the conclusion must be true. In the real world, however, arguments are messier.

It's true: George Square is in Edinburgh.

It's also true: I'm in George Square.

However, I'm *not* in Edinburgh. I'm in Glasgow.

I've just left Glasgow Queen Street train station and I'm currently sitting on a bench on George Square (the one in Glasgow). The point that I came here to make is this:

The argument above, in principle, is valid. If we assume that the first two statements are true, then the conclusion must be true. In logic, that's what 'validity' means. However, the validity of the argument depends on an assumption. It assumes that the term 'George

The limits of logic

Square' in the first two statements is the same thing. If it's not, then it's *not* a valid argument.

The problem isn't with logic. Logic is based on rules. To determine if the argument is valid, you need to assume that the first two statements are true. But logic doesn't tolerate ambiguity. If the terms in the statements are ambiguous – if they don't mean the same thing – then the argument doesn't work.

Logic is a formula: if this, then that. If *this* is true, then we can deduce *that*. The real world, however, is a messier place. We can't assume that any statement is true. We can't assume what's meant by 'this' or 'that'. Depending on the context, 'George Square' can mean different things.

Logical thinking can show how some arguments, in principle, are good or bad. It can help us to notice some of the assumptions that we make. It can point to some ambiguities. It can clear away some of the mess – but only some of it. The world of logical deduction is an abstract place, where rules are fixed and ambiguity is forbidden. The world in which we live, however, is ambiguous and uncertain.

It's time to go home now. The train departs at two o'clock. It takes forty-five minutes to reach Edinburgh. Therefore: I'll be home at 2.45.[1]

Ah, it seems that the train has been delayed ...

*

>All men are mortal.
>Socrates is a man.
>Therefore: Socrates is mortal.

Radical Thinking

This is the classic example of a form of argument: the syllogism. It consists of three statements: two premises and a conclusion. It's a valid argument because the conclusion follows from the premises. If Socrates is a man (premise 1) and all men are mortal (premise 2), then Socrates must be mortal (conclusion). And 'valid' just means that: if the premises are true, then the conclusion *must* be true. It doesn't matter if any of them are really true. It's a matter of form, not content. That's why it's called *formal* logic.

For example, this is equally valid:

> All men are potatoes.
> Socrates is a man.
> Therefore: Socrates is a potato.

Same form, different content. It's a *valid* argument because, *if* Socrates is a man *and* all men are potatoes, *then* Socrates must be a potato. It's not, however, a sound argument, because one of the premises is obviously untrue: in the real world, *not* all men are potatoes. Nevertheless, the argument is valid because, if we *assume* that the premises are true, then the conclusion *must* follow.

The logic is simple enough, if you follow the rules. For example:

> Some men are potatoes.
> Socrates is a man.
> Therefore: Socrates is a potato.

This is *not* a valid argument. If *some* men are potatoes *and* Socrates is a man, then it doesn't follow that he *must* be a potato. He might be one of those non-potato men. But sometimes arguments can be more deceptive. For example:

The limits of logic

Some Scots are Glaswegians.
Some Glaswegians are funny.
Therefore: Some Scots are funny.

This one seems valid. However, it's not. Think of the form, not the content:

Some Ss are Gs.
Some Gs are Fs.
Therefore: Some Ss are Fs.

This isn't valid because, if *some* Ss are Gs and *some* Gs are Fs, then it doesn't follow that some Ss *must* be Fs. The Ss that are Gs might not be Fs.

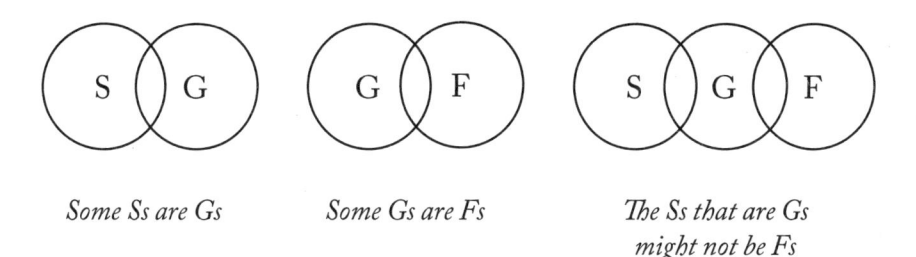

Some Ss are Gs　　　*Some Gs are Fs*　　　*The Ss that are Gs might not be Fs*

Nevertheless, when it has certain content (e.g. Some Scots are Glaswegians. Some Glaswegians are funny. Therefore: Some Scots are funny) it *does* seem valid. This is partly because the statements are true. We often confuse truth with validity. It's also because, simply in terms of logic, it *does* seem valid. After all, if some Glaswegians are funny, then surely some Scots must be funny?

However, there's a hidden assumption here: that all Glaswegians are Scots. This just seems obvious because we know that Glasgow

Radical Thinking

is a city in Scotland. However, the term 'Glaswegians' is ambiguous. It might refer to Glaswegians who aren't Scots. And, as it happens, there are plenty of them. There's even a Glasgow in Canada and there are several more in the United States.

In logic, ambiguous meanings are a problem. However, we can make these explicit. For example:

George Square is in Edinburgh. I'm in George Square. Therefore: I'm in Edinburgh.

We might translate this into the form:

GS is in E. P is in GS. Therefore: P is in E.

That's a valid argument.

However, if the first George Square isn't the same as the second George Square, then that would require a different form:

GS1 is in E. P is in GS2. Therefore: P is in E.

That's clearly *not* a valid argument.

The problem isn't with logic. The problem is in translating real-world arguments into the language of logic.[2] It's easy for things to get lost in translation. This is because real-world arguments are messier than logical arguments: depending on the context, 'George Square' can mean different things.

So, when we encounter a real-world claim, we need to know what it actually means.

In logic, ambiguous meanings are a problem. However, they can also suggest solutions. Take, for example, the paradox. There are

The limits of logic

many classic paradoxes which seem to be, well, paradoxical. One is the River of Heraclitus: you can't walk into same river twice. It's the same river yet not the same river. Another classic paradox is the Ship of Theseus: a ship that has every part of it gradually replaced until none of the original parts remain. It's the same ship yet a different ship.

We can make sense of these paradoxes, however, if we think about ambiguous meanings. The River of Heraclitus is a 'river', but that word can mean different things. If a river is a flow of water along a path, then it's the same river. If the river is the water itself, then that's always changing. It depends on the meaning of 'river'. The Ship of Theseus is a 'ship', but what does that mean? If it's the structure (called the Ship of Theseus), then it's the same ship. If it's the materials, then it's different. It depends on the meaning of 'ship'.

It also reveals the lack of a clear boundary between when 'a thing changes' and when 'a thing becomes a different thing'. A ship that has some of its parts replaced is basically the same ship. A ship that has all its parts replaced might be seen as a different ship. If the change is gradual, then it seems to be a slow transformation from 'old' to 'new'. But when does a new *version* of a thing become a *different* thing? There's no obvious boundary.

This can be seen in another classic paradox: 'The paradox of the heap'. If there's a heap of grain, then removing a single grain doesn't change it from being a heap. So, if you remove single grains, one at a time, until you're down to the final grain, then is this still a heap? According to the rule – removing a single grain doesn't change it from being a heap – there's no point at which it changes from being a heap to being a non-heap. So, when there's a single grain left, it must still be a heap.

Radical Thinking

George Square is currently busy. A single person leaving a busy space doesn't change it from being busy. If individuals continue to leave, one at a time, until there's only one person left, then is it still busy?

Same form, different content. But the answer seems obvious: if there's only one person left, then the square is *not* busy. That's not what 'busy' means. The rule – a single person leaving a busy space doesn't change it from being busy – may be true. But only in an abstract sense. In the real world, at some point, it doesn't work. It may be logical, but it makes no sense. Clearly, at some point, a line was crossed between 'busy' and 'not busy'. It's just that the line isn't obvious.

So, what to do? We could come up with rules. We could draw a boundary between 'busy' and 'not busy' – just to be clear about what we mean. For example, we could define 'busy' as 'fifty people or more'. Then, when there are only forty-nine people left, the square is no longer 'busy'. We could define a 'heap' as 'fifty grains or more'. Then, when there are only forty-nine grains left, it's no longer a 'heap'. We could come up with different rules, of course, and we might draw different boundaries.

However, we would need to draw particular boundaries. We would need to agree on the rules. We would need to be clear about what the terms mean. If we did that, then there would no ambiguity. We would know what was true. It would be obvious.

Meanwhile, behind the obvious truth, the less obvious things that make it true would remain. The boundaries that we draw. The rules that we follow. The assumptions that we make about what terms mean.

The limits of logic

In logic, the rules are clear. In the real world, they're not. So, how do the rules of logic relate to claims about the real world?

In Chapter 6, the original 'Critical Thinking' test was discussed, and an example question was given. It's now time to answer it, based on your knowledge of logic:

> All patriotic people are to be admired.
> No radicals are patriotic people.
> Therefore –
>   A. No radicals are to be admired.
>   B. All radicals are to be admired.
>   C. Some radicals are to be admired.
>   D. None of these conclusions necessarily follows.[3]

What do you think? Take a moment ...

Now, think of the form, not the content.

> All Ps are As.
> No Rs are Ps.
> Therefore:
>   A. No Rs are As.
>   B. All Rs are As.
>   C. Some Rs are As.
>   D. None of these conclusions necessarily follows.

If 'All Ps are As' and 'No Rs are Ps', then we don't know if any Rs are As. If all People are Alive and no Robots are People, then we don't know if any Robots are Alive. They *might* all be, or some, or none.

Radical Thinking

All Ps are As

No Rs are Ps

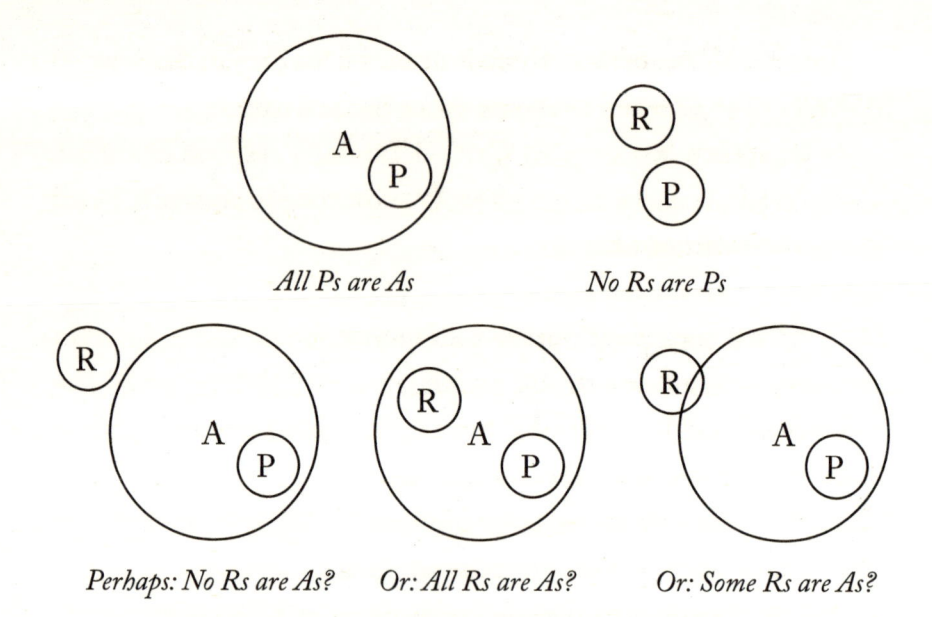

Perhaps: No Rs are As?   *Or: All Rs are As?*   *Or: Some Rs are As?*

However, none these conclusions *necessarily* follows. So, the correct answer is d.

If your answer was anything else, then that's an error. If you're new to the rules of logic, then it's an understandable error. However, if this is what you thought …

> All patriotic people are to be admired.
> No radicals are patriotic people.
> Therefore: No radicals are to be admired.

… then this is what probably happened:

You probably interpreted the first premise as 'All patriotic people (*and only them*) are to be admired'. But it doesn't follow from '*All patriotic people are to be admired*' that '*Only patriotic people are to be admired*'. If all Ps are As, then it doesn't follow that *only* Ps are As. After all, other things might be As too.

192

The limits of logic

This is a classic fallacy, which is usually described in this way:

If A, then B.
Not A.
Therefore: not B.[4]

It's a fallacy because it doesn't follow that, if all As are Bs, then nothing else is a B. It's the difference between a *sufficient* and a *necessary* condition. If something is an A, then that's *sufficient* for it be a B. However, that doesn't mean that, to be a B, it's *necessary* to be an A. In the case above, if you're a patriotic person, then that's sufficient (to be admired). But that doesn't mean that it's necessary.

This is according to the rules of logic – i.e. to be a valid argument, if the premises are assumed to be true, then the conclusion *must* follow from these. To avoid an error, you must follow the rules. The error is a breach of the rules. Or, to put it another way, the rules determine what's an error. So, if you know the rules and follow them, then you'll not make an error.

But, in the real world, you still don't know how many radicals are to be admired. The truth is probably c. Some radicals are to be admired (depending on what you mean by 'radical' and 'admired'). Different people, depending on what these words mean to them, might reach a different conclusion. In the real world, it's hard to separate form and content.

For example:

If you're eligible, then you're able to vote.
You're not eligible.
Therefore: you're unable to vote.

Radical Thinking

Same form, different content. So, this is also a fallacy. But it seems to be a valid argument because we think that, when it comes to voting, being 'eligible' is both sufficient *and* necessary. In the real-world context of voting, that makes sense. However, if we focus on the form, not the content, then we can see where the problem lies.

If E, then V.
Not E.
Therefore: not V.

Premise 1 (if E, then V) makes it a *sufficient* condition (if E, then that's sufficient for V). But that doesn't mean that it's *necessary*. Consider a slightly different content: if you're English, then you're able to vote. You're not English. Therefore: you're unable to vote. That's clearly a fallacy. The problem – the reason why the first version seems valid – is in the meaning of 'eligible'. We assume that it means 'eligible to vote'. But that's an assumption that we're making. After all, 'eligible' can mean different things. You might be an eligible bachelor. You might be an eligible customer.

If you follow the rules of formal logic, then you can notice when you're making assumptions and when you're being ambiguous. In the abstract world of formal logic, assumptions should be explicit, and ambiguity isn't tolerated. But this isn't the world in which we live, where assumptions and meanings depend on the context. You might indeed be 'eligible' in other ways. But that won't help at the polling station.

Applying the rules of formal logic to real-world arguments is a messy business. In the real world, assumptions are usually implicit. This is why they're not so obvious. When people make arguments, they play by different rules. In the process, ambiguity isn't merely tolerated: it's often deliberate. Real-world arguments mix form and content in ways that are harder to notice. How they do this depends on the context. They may exploit ambiguity. They may make things seem relevant when, logically speaking, they're not.

So, how can we apply the rules of logic to real-world knowledge claims?

Half a century ago, some philosophers thought that formal logic was too limited. So, they came up with a new kind of logic: Informal Logic. And, according to some, this was the essence of 'Critical Thinking'.[5]

They began to study the kinds of arguments that are made in the real world. They thought that formal logic was inadequate because it was concerned with the validity of arguments. It was concerned with form, not content. Informal logic was about everyday arguments, which always have content and context. It was concerned with the *soundness* of arguments (which depends on the premises being true). If the premises are true, then the argument is *sound*. And, to know if the premises are true, you need to consider the content and context.

Their primary concern was with the kinds of fallacious arguments that are used in everyday discourse. These fallacies appeared to be sound but were not. Philosophers identified a long list of these fallacies, and each of them was given a name. They've been described in many books, and they can easily be found online. If you're interested, then you can look them up. You can learn their names and, perhaps, if you know what they are, then you'll be able to spot them in the future. Perhaps.

Meanwhile, like the tools of persuasion, there are some common themes that are worth considering. These themes are related to content and context. In everyday arguments, the content matters, but often it's ambiguous. In everyday arguments, the context matters because, depending on the context, particular things will be relevant. Ambiguous meanings. Irrelevant arguments. These are two common themes.

There are several *fallacies of ambiguity*, when ambiguous meanings lead to error. We might think that what's true of a part of something must be true of the whole of it (the fallacy of *composition*). For example: Atoms are invisible to the human eye. Dogs are composed entirely of atoms. Therefore: dogs are invisible to the human eye. Or we might think that what's true of the whole of something is true of the parts of it (the fallacy of *division*). For example: My dog is black. His tongue is part of him. Therefore: his tongue is black. These are obvious errors, the result of confusing the part with the whole.

However, they're not always so obvious. For example, this error may be obvious: Arriving early will avoid queuing. Everyone is going. Therefore: if everyone arrives early, then they'll avoid queuing. But, depending on the context, this may not be so obvious: Owning a gun makes you feel safer. Everyone owns a gun. Therefore: everyone feels safer. The error is in assuming that what's true of the part must be true of the whole.

This error may be obvious: the British voted to leave the European Union. I am British. Therefore, I voted to leave the European Union. But, depending on the context, this may not be so obvious: Lower taxes make people better off. Taxes are being cut. Therefore: you'll be better off. The error is in assuming that what's true of the whole must be true of the parts of it.

The limits of logic

There are other fallacies of ambiguity. There is, for example, the fallacy of *equivocation*, which equates different things through ambiguous meaning. For example:

> Nothing is better than this.
> Anything is better than nothing.
> Therefore: anything is better than this.

In this case, the ambiguity is obvious: the word *nothing* can mean different things. So can *this*. Or *anything*. So, this argument could mean anything. Or nothing.

However, it's not always so obvious. In the real world, words are often ambiguous (because names can mean different things to different people). And it's not simply the ambiguity of words: it's the ambiguity of *meaning*. In certain contexts, different words with different meanings can be used as if they mean the same thing.

For example, a few years ago, when the Mayor of London described Donald Trump's views on Islam as 'ignorant', Trump responded by challenging the Mayor of London to an IQ test. In doing so, he equated 'ignorance' with 'IQ'. He did this because, to uninformed people, ignorance means the same as low intelligence. But ignorance is a lack of knowledge. IQ is a general ability. The most intelligent people in the world are ignorant about many things. The most intelligent person can be ignorant about Islam. Or, indeed, the least intelligent person.

This was, in practice, a fallacy of equivocation: he equated two things that mean different things. However, it was also a fallacy of irrelevance: in terms of the logic of the argument (about his 'ignorance' of Islam), his IQ was irrelevant.

Radical Thinking

There are several *fallacies of irrelevance*, when arguments are based on irrelevant matters. There's the *red herring*: it directs your attention to something that's irrelevant. There's the *straw man*: it distorts an argument to make it easier to attack. There's the *ad hominem*: it focuses on the flaws of an individual rather than flaws in what they're saying. There's the *tu quoque* ('you too') fallacy: rather than respond to an accusation, it makes a counter-accusation.

In practice, it can be hard to spot the differences. But they're all versions of a similar problem: rather than deal with the actual claim, they divert your attention to something else. Sometimes, these logical errors are obvious. When a politician is asked a question, they might talk about something else entirely (*red herring*). They might claim that limited gun control is about taking away your guns (*straw man*). They might accuse their opponent of being untrustworthy (*ad hominem*). And, if they're accused of lying or fraud, they might accuse others of doing the same thing (*tu quoque*).

At other times, it's not so obvious. For example, when the Mayor of London claimed that Trump's views on Islam were 'ignorant', Trump's responses were a confusing mixture of fallacies – *straw men*, *red herrings*, *tu quoques* and *ad hominems* – that were irrelevant to the actual accusation. But that didn't particularly matter. They weren't supposed to be a *logical* response. They were a *political* response to manage the accusation. And, in *that* sense, they weren't irrelevant. They helped him to manage the accusation that his views about Islam were ignorant.

In real-world arguments, we can identify logical fallacies, and we can give them names. They're errors in terms of the logic of the argument. And, if we can spot them, then they're useful reminders of how we can be misled. But, in practice, they have their limits. Logical fallacies may lead to erroneous outcomes, but we need to think about the process. And, in real-world arguments, there's a bigger picture to the process: there are other things going on beyond the mere logic of an argument.

When people make claims about this or that, they present a *particular* picture. They describe some things, not others, and they describe them in a particular way. This doesn't mean that what they say is wrong. Nevertheless, by making particular things relevant, and by doing so in an ambiguous way, this can shape our thoughts.

They can *imply* a fact without stating it explicitly. For example, the old advert: Most Doctors Smoke Camels. It may be a fact that most doctors smoke Camels. It may also be a fact that most plumbers smoke Camels. But only one of these facts implies something else. And it does so without stating it explicitly.

It's not simply a case of which facts to choose. The same fact, described in a particular way, can do similar work. It can insinuate, or it can avoid an insinuation. For example, this is from a legal trial, when discussing the place where the victim of an alleged rape met the accused:

Defence counsel.   It's where girls and fellas meet, isn't it?
Alleged victim: People go there.[6]

It may be a fact that she went to this place 'where girls and fellas meet'. Or where 'people go'. However, in the context of a rape trial, the first description insinuates something. The second description avoids it. When particular facts are described in particular ways, this can suggest responsibility.

For example, this is from a discussion about a strange noise outside a shared flat:

A. [There's] something outside. It was definitely outside.
D. Neil, you've got shoes on.⁷

It may be true that Neil has shoes on. It may be true that Neil has socks on. But only one of these facts implies something else. It does so without making it explicit. It might have been explicit (Neil, I think you should check it out), but that might have provoked an obvious response (Why don't *you* check it out?). Instead, it makes a particular fact relevant. It makes an argument in an ambiguous way. This makes it harder to challenge.

Ambiguous meanings may lead to error, but they also serve a practical function: they make arguments harder to challenge. The vaguer the claim, the harder it is to challenge it. Meanwhile, it quietly implies something else. *It is what it is.* Who can argue with that? Meanwhile, it implies that nothing can be done. *He's not the smartest guy in the world.* This is true of all guys, except one. Meanwhile, it implies that this guy is stupid. *There's definitely something going on. You know what they say. No smoke without fire.* If you wish to imply that something is the case, then sometimes smoke is all you need.

Irrelevant arguments may be fallacious but, depending on the context, they're not entirely irrelevant. The *ad hominem* may be illogical but, if somebody expects to be believed, then their personal character *is* relevant. The *tu quoque* may be illogical but, when somebody makes an accusation, it matters if they're guilty of the same thing. It may be irrelevant to the logic of the argument but, in terms of the bigger picture, it *does* matter. It matters if people are untrustworthy. It matters if people are hypocrites.

In the real world, we can look at the logic of any argument. However, we need to know what, precisely, *is* the argument. This can be difficult to spot, because there are other things going on. It may be ambiguous, but that may not be an error. It may be irrelevant to *this*, but not to *that*. It may be an attempt to change the conversation: to get us to focus on the truth of *that*, so that we stop thinking about *this*. Whatever the content, there's always a context, and, depending on the context, different things may be relevant. If we don't understand the context, then we won't understand why they're making *that* relevant.

If we wish to make sense of what's going on, then logic only gets us so far. Whatever the claim might happen to be, we need to begin with what they really *mean*. And we need to think about the *purpose*: why, of all the things that they might say, are they telling us *that*?

We also need to think about the *basis* of the claim: not only the evidence, but also the assumptions, on which it's based. After all, even in science, facts are always limited, and they need to be interpreted. Scientific thinking, like logical thinking, is remarkably useful, but it has its limits.

So, let's consider the boundaries of science.

11

The boundaries of science

In 1824, George Combe announced that he'd discovered Wonder.[1]

He did this at the first meeting of the Edinburgh Phrenological Society, which was the first phrenological society in the world. They didn't have a headquarters yet, so they met at Combe's house. He lived on Brown's Square, named after James Brown, the same architect who designed George Square. Brown's Square was demolished about 150 years ago. Today, above where it used to be – where George Combe discovered Wonder – is the Elephant House café: the 'birthplace' of Harry Potter.

The Edinburgh Phrenological Society also came to an end about 150 years ago. Nevertheless, phrenology is still a useful reminder of the boundaries of science. And, if we're going to think in a 'scientific' way, then we need to remember its limits.

George Combe was converted by the apostle of phrenology, Johann Spurzheim, who'd visited Edinburgh a few years earlier. According to Spurzheim, your brain is divided into thirty-three distinct organs. Each one determines a part of your character. For example, there's an organ of Destructiveness (which determines how aggressive you

The boundaries of science

are) and an organ of Amativeness (which determines your sexual drive). The latter is located in the cerebellum, at the base of the back of your skull. According to Spurzheim, a bump in that location indicates a large organ of Amativeness beneath the skull.

When people learn about this, they often feel the back of their heads.

If only out of curiosity.

Phrenology became popular in the nineteenth century. It appeared to offer a way to understand individual character. According to phrenology, everyone had the same thirty-three organs, but they weren't the same size. It was the combination of the relative sizes that determined your individual character. It was based on comparing the sizes of particular organs with (what they thought was) the character of certain people. For example, according to phrenology, murderers had an excessively large organ of Destructiveness, and a large organ of Amativeness was a feature of rabbits, but not of women.[2]

It had all begun with Franz Gall, the father of phrenology. Gall had collected a large number of skulls and had compared their shapes to what he knew about their original owners. He'd observed that the skulls of murderers had a bump in the same location. He'd believed that this was no coincidence: that these skulls had housed similar brains. He believed that, since the shape of the skull was parallel to the shape of the brain, the skull of a murderer had a bump in that location because there had been a large organ beneath it. And that organ reflected his character. Gall had named this the organ of Murder. It was an organ that everyone possessed but, in most people, it was too small to be significant. In the case of a few (such as, say, murderers), it was a dominant part of their character. In

Radical Thinking

the same way, Gall had found that poets had a large organ of Poetic Talent and that musicians had a large organ of Music.

Gall had taught this to Spurzheim. Later, Spurzheim changed the names. He renamed the organ of Murder: Destructiveness. He chose the name Amativeness to replace the coarser original: Impulse to Propagation. Spurzheim also added a few organs that he felt were missing. Gall, for example, hadn't found an organ of Hope. However, Spurzheim felt that there should be a place for Hope. So, he added it to his list of phrenological organs and made a space for it – just in front of Conscientiousness and below Veneration. Which sounds oddly appropriate.

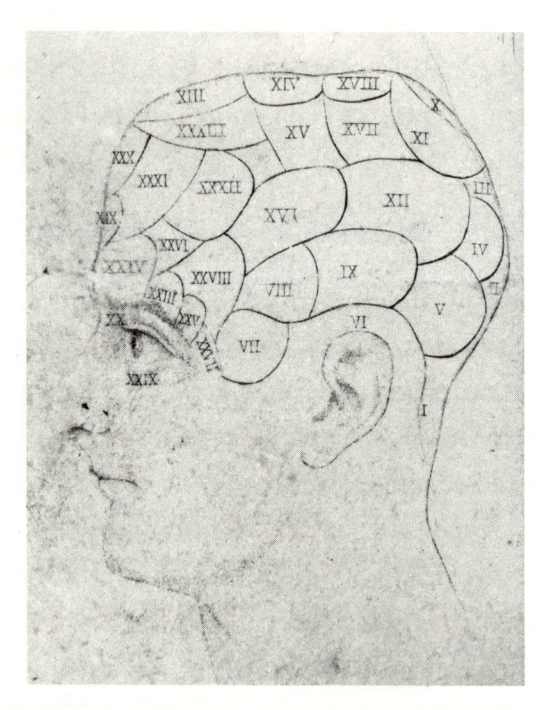

Spurzheim's map of the brain. If you're looking for Hope, then you'll find it at number XV. However, just in front of Hope, there's a blank space. What could it represent?

Spurzheim drew new boundaries on the cranial map. He gave new names to the territories. He then wrote a book on the subject and travelled around giving lectures on it. The book included his map of the brain, which was divided into his new categories. However, if you looked at Spurzheim's map of the brain, then you might have noticed that something was missing. Just below Imitation was a blank space. It sat in front of Hope and behind Wit. This blank space seemed to represent a particular organ of the brain. However, what it represented was a mystery.

In 1824, the mystery was solved. At a meeting of the Edinburgh Phrenological Society, George Combe made an announcement: the blank space represented an organ that was prominent in people who were 'fond of novelty, and susceptible of vivid emotions of surprise'.[3] He gave it a name: the organ of Wonder. Later, Spurzheim changed the name. He called it the organ of Marvellousness. To him, 'wonder' meant something else.[4]

To others, however, there was nothing marvellous about phrenology. So, they gave it other names. Pierre Roget, who published the *Thesaurus*, called it 'frivolous' and 'ridiculous'.[5] Francis Jeffrey, the literary critic, described phrenology as 'a very fantastical and ... most absurd hypothesis'.[6] François Magendie, the most eminent physiologist in Europe, used a new word to describe phrenology: he called it 'pseudo-science'.[7]

Since then, the original pseudoscience has continued to be the target of debunking. Debunkers have used it to draw a boundary between science and pseudoscience. They've pointed to phrenology as a typical case of uncritical (pseudoscientific) thinking. They're not entirely wrong. But they're not entirely right.

If we think in a less obvious way about the original pseudoscience,

Radical Thinking

then we can see that the boundary between science and non-science is fuzzy. We can see that science is based not only on evidence, but also on making assumptions about how to interpret the evidence. We can also see that, despite its limits – indeed, *because* of its limits – scientific thinking is so useful.

When Spurzheim came to Edinburgh, it was to defend his reputation. An anonymous review of his book had just appeared in the *Edinburgh Review*, a highly influential journal at the time. The reviewer had exhibited Destructiveness, not Amativeness. He'd denounced the book as 'a mixture of gross errors, extravagant absurdities, downright misstatements, and unmeaning quotations from Scripture'.[8] So, Spurzheim came to Edinburgh to confront the anonymous reviewer.

When he arrived, he gave a series of lectures at the University of Edinburgh. In these, he dissected brains in front of some of the most eminent anatomists of the time. This included the anonymous reviewer, who revealed himself to be John Gordon, a widely respected expert on brain anatomy. There was, not surprisingly, a heated exchange between the two. However, according to the press, the audience was 'unquestionably in favour of Dr Spurzheim, in the proportion of at least twenty to one'.[9] The boundary between science and pseudoscience, as far as these experts were concerned, wasn't obvious.

The private letters of the phrenologist also show that he was delighted with how it had gone. George Combe was convinced by what he saw and heard, and became a convert. Spurzheim was also confident that he'd converted many others. In a letter to his wife-to-be, he declared: 'It is astonishing how I have gained in the public opinion since my lecturing ... it [i.e. phrenology] is no longer quackery, but an important science.'[10]

That turned out to be an example of Hope prevailing over Cautiousness. The controversy continued and, as it continued, each side appealed to the facts. However, the facts, even when they could be seen with their own eyes, could be interpreted in different ways. In one attempt to settle the matter, brains were dissected and observed. However, this didn't settle the matter. When Spurzheim and Gordon looked at the dissected brains, they disagreed about what they saw.

For example, when a brain was cut with a scalpel, the tissue appeared to be smooth. However, if the brain tissue was scraped, then it appeared to be fibrous. Gordon claimed that cutting with a scalpel was the correct way to observe the structure of brain tissue. Spurzheim claimed that the tissue had to be scraped to reveal its real structure.[11] They observed the same thing, but their interpretations differed: they were based on different assumptions about how best to observe the brain.

So, the controversy continued. Phrenologists assumed that the brain was the seat of the mind and that it was divided into different organs. However, some critics debunked phrenology on the grounds that the mind was independent of the brain. Other debunkers of phrenology believed that the mind couldn't be divided up. The most common criticism of phrenology at the time was that it made no room for the soul and, therefore, was a challenge to Christian faith.

Today, however, very few scientists would claim that the mind is independent of the brain. Very few scientists would now be troubled by the idea that science challenges religious faith. And, according to contemporary neuroscience, different parts of the brain are indeed responsible for specific functions. In other words, based on these points, scientists would now side with the phrenologists, not the critics. In fact, phrenology can be seen as a pioneer of some key ideas that became accepted in psychology and neuroscience.[12]

Since then, of course, there have been more sophisticated observations and we've learned considerably more about the brain. There are precious few phrenologists now. However, those familiar images of a scanned brain, with coloured blobs in specific places, aren't direct observations. They're pictorial representations of data, which are based on changes in particular kinds of brain activity in response to certain questions and tasks. What they mean continues to depend on making assumptions about what's observed.

The limits of neuroscience are the limits of any science. Scientific observations must be interpreted, and how this is done depends on the relevant theory and method of observation. The claims of scientists, like the claims of anyone, are based on limited observations and on making assumptions about what these mean. After all, scientists are people too. So, drawing a clear line between Science and Pseudoscience has never been easy.

For example, in the seventeenth century, scientific knowledge was regarded as certain. It was thought to be based on objective facts and independent of theory or opinion. However, as scientific knowledge changed over time, it became clear that it wasn't certain. In the nineteenth century, some defined science in terms of 'the scientific method'. However, even among experts, there was disagreement about what this was. In the twentieth century, philosophers of science tried to draw a clearer boundary. They claimed that science was based on verification: a scientific theory must be *verified* by observation. However, too many dodgy theories could also be verified by observation. After all, when phrenologists observed skulls and brains, they found evidence that confirmed their theory.

So, in the mid-twentieth century, a new boundary was drawn. Karl Popper, the philosopher of science, admitted that the earlier boundaries were inadequate. Science wasn't certain. It wasn't based on 'the scientific method'. It wasn't about *verifying* a claim by observation. On the contrary, it was about trying to *falsify* it. The aim of science was to test a theory or claim in order to prove it wrong. So, if it wasn't falsifiable by observation – if there were no facts that could show it to be wrong – then it wasn't scientific. That was a better way to distinguish between science and non-science. However, even that boundary was inadequate. For one thing, any dodgy theory could be falsified by observation. Furthermore, when scientists made observations, these observations were limited, and they had to be interpreted. In the process, the observed facts could be compatible with different theories. And, in the practice of science, when facts were observed that didn't fit with a theory, the theory wasn't necessarily discarded.

For example, when astronomers observed that the movements of Uranus weren't in line with Newtonian theory, they still held on to the theory. They supposed that this could be explained by the existence of a more distant planet, which they couldn't observe. It was only later that they observed the planet (and, when they did, they named it Neptune). In hindsight, this was good science. At the time, however, they held onto the theory despite the observable facts. So, whatever science was, it wasn't simply a matter of falsification.

The boundary between science and pseudoscience remains fuzzy.[13] However, that doesn't mean that anything goes. The boundaries may have changed over time. They may have been based on

Radical Thinking

making particular distinctions between this and that. Nevertheless, these distinctions matter. And one in particular.

It's why phrenology continues to be a target of debunkers of pseudoscience. As we'll now see, however, if you want to think in a scientific way, then knowing about it isn't enough: you need to do it.

It remains a core part of scientific thinking: test a claim in a way that might falsify it. In the scientific world, tests are conducted in controlled conditions, using particular methods of observation, and the analysis of data follows specific rules. In the real world, of course, conditions are noisy and there are different ways to interpret what we observe. This doesn't prevent us from looking for evidence that might show our beliefs to be wrong. However, we tend not to do that.

This tendency has been known for centuries. In 1620, Francis Bacon, the pioneer of scientific thinking, pointed out that 'human understanding when it has once adopted an opinion … draws all things else to support and agree with it. And though there be a greater number and weight of instances to be found on the other side, yet these it either neglects and despises, or else by some distinction sets aside and rejects [them].'[14] Even then, it was hardly a new idea. More than two thousand years ago, the Greek historian Thucydides pointed out that 'it is a habit of mankind to entrust to careless hope what they long for, and to use sovereign reason to thrust aside what they do not fancy.'[15]

Nor was this tendency forgotten. In the nineteenth century, it was well known. Henry Maudsley, the famous English psychiatrist, described 'the well-known tendency of the mind, so much insisted on by Bacon, to be impressed vividly by agreeing instances and to

The boundaries of science

remember them, while overlooking and forgetting the opposing instances'.[16] In 1941, one of the authors of the original Critical Thinking test made the same point: one of the 'causes of errors in thinking', he explained, is the 'failure to note negative evidence ... favorable cases are noted, and the others forgotten'.[17]

So, we've known about this tendency for a very long time.

However, in 1960, a famous experiment was conducted. At the time, Karl Popper had just drawn his boundary between science and pseudoscience: the former attempted to falsify a theory. And this well-known tendency – to seek *confirming* evidence – was the opposite of that. So, if this was how we really thought, then we didn't think in a scientific way. However, nobody had tested this. The aim of the experiment was to find out if we really think in an unscientific way.

In this experiment, subjects were told that a sequence of numbers (2 – 4 – 6) followed a simple rule. Their task was to discover the rule. They were to try new sequences of numbers. They were to explain their reasons for choosing them. For example, many tried the sequence: 8 – 10 – 12. Their theory was that the rule for 2 – 4 – 6 might be 'increasing even numbers'. However, when they did this, they were told that this was *not* the rule. So, they continued until they discovered the rule. The experiment showed that, when subjects tried to test their theory about what the rule might be, they tended to try sequences that were designed to confirm the theory (for example, if they thought that the rule might be 'increasing even numbers', then they tried a sequence that might confirm this, such as: 8 – 10 – 12).[18]

The experiment confirmed the well-known tendency. Of course, it might have falsified it. They might have found that subjects looked for *disconfirming* evidence. If that had happened, then the experiment would have led to negative results. That's what made it science. However, like all science, it was based on limited facts, which had to be interpreted. We need to remember its limits.

For example, there were only twenty-nine subjects. In terms of the outcome, all of them discovered the rule, and almost all of them did so within three tries. In terms of the process, few of them *spontaneously* looked for disconfirming evidence. However, most of them did – *at some point* – look for disconfirming evidence. So, the facts might have been interpreted differently: as evidence that we often *do* think in a scientific way.

In any case, the experiment became famous, and has been described as 'the first experiment that showed people to be illogical and irrational'.[19] Later, more experiments were conducted, which provided evidence that confirmed this tendency to seek confirming evidence. This tendency was given a name: 'confirmation bias'. Since then, 'confirmation bias' has become the embodiment of unscientific thinking. In the ever-expanding list of errors that we make, it has remained at the top. It's seen as the opposite of scientific thinking, and as the cause of erroneous outcomes. It's seen as a cause of belief in superstition, paranormal phenomena and conspiracy theories. As the old joke goes: once you learn about confirmation bias, you can find evidence of it everywhere.

The tendency is now better known than ever. Nevertheless, we continue to do it. When it's first pointed out, of course, we take notice. And then we carry on as normal: noticing things that confirm what we think and ignoring things that don't. This can lead to erroneous outcomes. When this happens, it's far from obvious.

In an attempt to make it more obvious, debunkers of pseudoscience have continued to debunk phrenology. They've pointed out that, if phrenologists found evidence that didn't fit with their beliefs, then this was explained away.[20] Meanwhile, phrenologists accepted evidence, without questioning it, when it supported their beliefs. There's a famous story, which has been cited by debunkers. Spurzheim was invited to the home of François Magendie (the French physiologist) to examine the preserved brain of Laplace (the great French polymath). Before he arrived, however, Magendie secretly switched the brain of Laplace with the brain of an imbecile. When Spurzheim saw it, he admired the brain as if it had belonged to a great polymath.[21]

This is a nice little piece of debunking. It's been used, more than once, to illustrate how phrenologists were uncritical thinkers: they accepted evidence, without questioning it, when it was in line with their beliefs. But debunking isn't scientific thinking. For example, if you didn't already believe that phrenology was nonsense, then you might wonder if the story is true. You might, for example, check the evidence.

If you bother to check it, then you discover that the story was told by another French physiologist, M. J. P. Flourens. Flourens was one of the most hostile enemies of phrenology. He regarded phrenologists as 'fair game for all kinds of demeaning practical jokes'.[22] That's why he told the story, which is entirely without support.[23] But if you didn't bother to check the evidence, then you might believe that it actually happened. In a more curious sense, then, the story really does illustrate how we accept evidence, without questioning it, when it supports our beliefs.

The problem of debunking is rather like the problem of phrenology. Once we're convinced that we're right, we stop questioning our own assumptions. We fail to look for evidence that doesn't fit.

We might know all about 'confirmation bias'. We might know that it's 'unscientific'. But this doesn't make us immune to it.

This is the thing about scientific thinking: you need to do it.

So, how do we do it?

Scientists have been trying to limit their own biases for a long time. They've done this as part of an ongoing quest for objectivity and truth. However, unlike fundamentalists, they no longer pretend to absolute truth. There was a time when they did, but they changed their minds. They were persuaded by negative evidence. They've accepted that, while absolute truth is appealing, it's not available. There's observable evidence, which is always limited and must be interpreted, so nothing is certain. And, if further evidence suggests something else, then it's time to change your mind.

Meanwhile, scientists have come up with ways to manage the problem of bias. There's a famous example from the history of astronomy. By the early nineteenth century, astronomers had noticed that their observations differed. When they looked through a telescope to observe the movement of stars — specifically, at what precise moment a star reached a specific position — they came up with slightly different measurements. This was, in part, because they had to react to an event — the moment at which a star crossed a line on the lens of a telescope — and individuals reacted differently.

So, a practical solution was created. If astronomers were observing the same thing, but observing it in a different way, then these differences could be compared. These differences became known as 'personal equations': personal biases in how individuals observed. When they made observations, their 'personal equation' could be factored in, and their observations could be compared to those of others.

The 'personal equation' came to be seen as a source of error. But it wasn't 'error' in the sense of 'wrong'. It wasn't a deviation from the truth. It was a difference in how individuals observed. The observation of a star continued to depend on the observer's judgement, which depended on comparing the position of a star to the position of a line on a lens. There was no independent access to the truth. However, in the absence of absolute truth, they could draw on a range of perspectives. And, within this bigger picture, alternative perspectives could be understood.

Later, psychologists began to study how people observe reality. They studied how long it takes for people to react to what they see and hear. They studied how long it takes to discriminate between one thing and another. And they studied how accurately we see things. When they began to do this, however, they had direct access to the truth. They had subjects judge the length of a line (or the distance between two shapes) and found that subjects were often inaccurate. These errors were explained in terms of 'personal equations' and other forms of bias. In this case, however, they were *actual* errors. Since psychologists knew the *true* length of the line (or the *true* distance between two shapes), they knew whether, and to what extent, subjects were getting it wrong.

However, as was pointed out at the time, these perceptual biases were different from biases 'which influence personal opinion of men and events'.[24] Outside the laboratory, there were other factors – such as what people noticed, and how open-minded they were to alternative views – which shaped their thoughts. These other kinds of bias, it was felt, were unavoidable and unpredictable.[25] After all, when we form opinions about people and events, we rarely, if ever, really know what's true.

If you *know* the truth, of course, such as the length of a line (or the distance between two shapes), then you can spot an error. You can see how far we stray from the truth. However, when the truth is uncertain, you can observe variations in judgement. You can then compare these and spot the differences. And, when you form opinions about people and events, this provides a bigger picture in which you can understand different perspectives.

The problem is that, when we *think* that we know the truth, we assume that others are in error. We think that *their* beliefs are the result of bias. This is convenient. It confirms what we think. However, we're all prone to bias.

So, we need to remember our own limits.

Psychologists often remind us of our limits. They've discovered many biases to which we're prone, and they've told us about them. It's a long list and, over the decades, it's grown. We've been told that these biases distort our thinking and lead to erroneous conclusions.[26] In short, bias is a cause of error.

However, in the real world – where we can't be certain about the truth – we can't know if we've made an error. When we arrive at a particular conclusion, we can't be certain about the outcome. We can, however, think about the process. In the case of confirmation bias, it's a deviation from scientific thinking: we tend to seek confirming evidence, rather than disconfirming evidence. So, we can try to avoid this. We can look for evidence that doesn't fit with what we already think. We can consider alternative perspectives. Even if we do, of course, we'll never be certain that we got it right. The problem of bias, in the real world, isn't that we get things wrong: it's that we forget our limits.

We're biased, in various ways, and we need to remember this. And scientists are people too. However, they've come up with ways to limit their biases. They can do this in a particular context: in controlled conditions, they can test the effects of this versus that. If they do *this*, then one thing happens. If they do *that*, then another thing happens. They can compare the two and spot the differences. In the real world, we can rarely control the conditions. But there are times that we can, and times that we do think in a scientific way.

For example, you're sitting by a table lamp, and the light goes out. You think that the bulb has blown. You replace the bulb, but it doesn't work either – you think that your theory was wrong. Perhaps it's the lamp? You might try another lamp, but, if it doesn't work either, then you think that your theory was wrong. Or perhaps it's the socket? You might try the lamp in a different socket but, if it still doesn't work, then you think that your theory was wrong. Perhaps it's the fuse? So, you try different switches, and you check the fuse box. In other words, you test different theories and, when the evidence doesn't fit, you change your mind. You come to conclusions based on 'trial and error', which is basic scientific thinking, and where 'error' isn't a problem: it's part of the process.

However, when we form opinions about people and events, it's messier than that. We can't control the conditions. We can't test to see if this leads to that. But we can collect the available data to get a sense of the bigger picture. In the case of some events, we can find out their overall probability (for example, how frequently they tend to happen), which provides a useful perspective. And, as individuals, we can be more aware of the ways in which our thoughts are shaped by common tendencies that, in general, we have. If we're aware of these biases, whether or not they lead to error, this can be a useful reminder of our limits. It can help us to think about what we're missing.

For example, there's a famous story, which is often embellished, but these are the facts. During the Second World War, American bombers were being shot down. The military wanted to reinforce the planes. Since reinforcements added weight to the plane, they wanted to reinforce only the most vulnerable parts. Their initial thought was to reinforce the parts of returning planes that showed the most hits. That seemed obvious. However, Abraham Wald, a mathematician, thought in a less obvious way. He assumed (on the basis of good evidence) that hits on planes would be evenly distributed. The planes that survived, therefore, were probably *not* hit in the most vulnerable parts: it was the ones that did *not* return that were hit in the most vulnerable parts.[27] So, he advised that planes should be reinforced in the parts that showed the *least* hits. He came up with a less obvious conclusion: by thinking about what was missing.

This became the classic example of overcoming the so-called 'survivorship bias': we tend to focus on the survivors, while ignoring the ones that didn't make it. It's easy to find examples of it. It can be found in decisions to start a business, because *this* kind of business appears to succeed – but what about the many that didn't? It can be found in histories of 'progress', which explain how we reached our present position – while ignoring the routes that we might have taken. It can be found in countless books on how to be successful, which rely on the wisdom of successful people. They attribute their success to hard work and perseverance, to learning from mistakes, making the right decisions, and other obvious things. They imply that, if you do the same things, then you'll also be successful. Many others did these things yet failed. But nobody seeks advice from those who failed.

'Survivorship bias' is a reminder of what we're missing. There's a bigger picture beyond what we currently see. There are quiet failures and lost causes. There are options that were once available, and there are routes that we might have taken. There are countless things that we don't notice because, here and now, they're no longer available.

Even psychological scientists, who look for evidence of failure – evidence that might *falsify* a particular position – have been prone to a similar bias. A tendency to publish successful results, rather than unsuccessful ones, led to a 'publication bias'. Some studies survived the process of publication and some didn't. Results that failed to reproduce previous findings were considered insignificant. Results that *merely* reproduced previous findings were considered irrelevant. This shaped the content of scientific knowledge: it ignored what seemed insignificant or irrelevant.

However, as this was brought to their notice, scientists gradually changed their minds. There has been a recent shift in scientific thinking: to publish failures as well as successes, to make available what was once invisible because it seemed insignificant or irrelevant.

This is the thing about scientific thinking. There are ways to manage bias, but knowing about them isn't enough. You need to do it.

When we talk about bias, what are we talking about?

Phrenologists talked about Hope and Cautiousness. We now have the Optimism Bias and the Pessimism Bias. Phrenologists talked about Inhabitiveness (which produces the desire to stay where you are). Now we have the Status Quo Bias. Phrenologists talked about Self-Love. Now we have the Self-serving Bias. Phrenologists talked about these tendencies as things that we all have, albeit in different amounts. However, when psychologists talk about biases, they're often presented as distortions and errors, rather than as common tendencies.

We can certainly find examples of common tendencies that we have, and we can give them names. When we seek advice from successful people, we might call this 'survivorship bias'. When they find examples of successful things that they did, we might call this 'confirmation bias'. However, these may not be errors: the advice may be useful, they may have done the right things, and they may have cited (what they think) are the most useful examples. It's simply that the outcome isn't guaranteed.

When we think of bias as a deviation from the truth, we're assuming that we know the truth. But we can think about the process, not the outcome. In the messy world of people and events, we don't have access to absolute truth, so we can never be certain when (or to what extent) biases lead to error. Even in science, observations are limited and must be interpreted, because scientists are people too. So, they make claims based on the available evidence, and by making assumptions about what it means. Science is a process, which leads to outcomes, but these outcomes aren't set in stone.

That's why scientific knowledge changes. Scientists used to think *that*. They now think *this*. In hindsight, *that* seems like an error. But *that* was based on the available evidence. They looked for new evidence, which was previously missing, and, when they found it, they changed their minds. These are the limits to scientific thinking. They're *precisely* what make it so useful.

Scientific thinking isn't a specific thing. Any scientific claim is based on the question that's asked, the evidence that's collected, and how that evidence is interpreted. However, there are some common themes and, in terms of critical thinking, they're useful. One is that, whatever you might think is the case, you should try to show it to be wrong. What the 1960 experiment showed is that we tend not to do this, though sometimes we do, but it's rarely a default position. In general, we tend to look for evidence that confirms what we think. And, here and now, we tend to call this 'confirmation bias'.

So, whatever we currently think, we need to consider alternative views, and we need to think about what we're missing. We need to look at what, according to *our* view, might seem insignificant or irrelevant. And, if we find evidence that we've previously ignored, then we can weigh up the options. We can compare the two and spot the differences. We can be prepared to change our minds.

Whatever we think – whatever we might see or hear – whatever the knowledge claim that we embrace, or that we might encounter – we need to think about its *basis*. After all, even in science, evidence is always limited, and it's based on certain assumptions. If we remember our limits, then we'll get a better sense of the bigger picture. We might then have a bit more humility, be more tolerant of the views of others, and be more suspicious of those who pretend to Truth. We might think in a more critical way.

However, we need to do it.

To do it, whatever the claim might be, we need to begin with what it *means*. We need to think about the *basis* of the claim: the evidence, and the assumptions, on which it's based. We also need to think about the *purpose*: why, of all the things that they might say, are they telling us *this*?

If we do that, then we can make sense of anything.

12

You can make sense of anything

Let's begin with the facts.

I'm in George Square. It's raining.

These are facts. If they're true. Facts, of course, are supposed to be true. In the real world, however, nothing is certain. We don't see the world as it *really* is. We have no direct access to absolute truth. That's why we need to *make* sense of things. So, how do we do that?

'It's raining' *describes* a reality: drops of water are falling from above. We've given this reality a name: 'rain'. Rain is real. 'It's raining' is a fact. Assuming, of course, that it's true. And, right now, it's true. It *is* raining.

This reality might be described in other ways. It might be 'spitting' or 'drizzling' or 'pouring'. It might be a 'shower' or a 'deluge'. And *this*, right now, seems more like a shower. Nevertheless, there's a reality to it: either it's raining or else it's not. It wasn't raining earlier. It is now.

But when did it change from one thing to another? Was it when the first drop fell? Is a single drop sufficient to count as 'rain'? Or do we need more? How many: fifty? There's no obvious boundary. Still, at some point, it became a fact: it *is* raining. Though only here and now. It's not raining everywhere. And *this* rain began at different times elsewhere.

So, it's raining. That *is* a fact. In this context (here and now). Depending on what we mean by 'rain'.

But how do I know? It looks like rain, though, I suppose, it might be a special effect (sometimes they make films in Edinburgh). But that seems highly improbable. And, of course, I might be dreaming. Or it may be a memory: by the time that you read this, it may not be raining. Come to think of it, it's *already* a memory. I can't see the rain right now, because I'm typing this. But I saw it a moment ago. Hang on, let me just check that it's still ... OK, *now* it's stopped. But it *was* raining. Well, almost certainly, here and ... then. Though memory is notoriously unreliable.

So, it *is* a fact: it *was* raining. In *this* context. Depending on what we mean by 'rain'. *And* assuming that my memory is reliable.

But how do *you* know that it's a fact? I'm telling you this, but I might be wrong. You need to trust that I'm honest and competent: that I'm a reliable source. You need to trust the evidence that I provide.

A fact is a claim that tells us something about the world. Whatever it describes, it refers to a particular context. Whatever it describes, it's based on words that have meanings: it depends on what they *mean*. It may be true, but that depends on the reliability of the evidence that supports it. That's the *basis* of the claim.

Meanwhile, of course, there are countless facts. I'm in George Square. It's raining. I'm in the office. I don't have an umbrella. I'm waiting until it stops. You're reading this. You're breathing. There are endless other facts about all of us, at every moment, wherever we

Radical Thinking

happen to be. So, we can't begin with *all* the facts. We need to begin with *particular* facts. But which ones? There are so many options.

How do we choose between alternative facts?

A few years ago, there was a curious debate about the existence of alternative facts. Some claimed that they were real. Others claimed that they were falsehoods. Whether or not there are 'alternative facts', however, depends on what you mean. And that requires some context.

It began in 2017, just after the election of Donald Trump. Following the inauguration ceremony, Sean Spicer – the first of Trump's White House press secretaries – criticised the media for underestimating attendance at the ceremony. He claimed that it had attracted the 'largest audience to ever witness an inauguration, period'.

He backed up this claim with some facts.[1] For example, on the day of Trump's inauguration, 420,000 people rode the Washington DC Metro. However, in 2013, on the day of President Obama's inauguration, the figure had been a mere 317,000. These facts supported the claim: the attendance in 2017 was larger.

The claim was based on particular facts: the DC Metro data for 2017 versus 2013. These were interpreted in a certain way: as evidence of attendance at an inauguration ceremony. There's nothing wrong with that (assuming, of course, that the facts are true). However, the claim wasn't about 2017 versus 2013: it was about 'ever'. If we want to check the *actual* claim, then we need to look farther. And, as it happens, we needn't look far.

According to DC Metro data, the figure for 2013 was correct (for the period between 0000 and 1100: it was 317,000). However,

You can make sense of anything

in 2009, on Obama's *first* inauguration day, the figure (for the same time period) was 513,000. So, Trump's audience was *not* the largest ever.

This claim is also based on particular facts: the DC Metro data for the period between 0000 and 1100. There are other facts that might be used, but these are the ones that Spicer used to support *his* claim. It makes the same assumptions: that the particular facts are true, and that we treat them as evidence of attendance at an inauguration ceremony. So, we can compare the two and spot the differences. Whatever the *true* attendance was, Spicer's claim – that this was the largest ever – was based on cherry-picking the facts.

This is a common problem: we can often find facts that support a particular view. That's why we need to look farther: to look for evidence that might falsify a claim.

However, this isn't why Spicer's claim became famous. After all, according to his facts, attendance in 2017 (420,000) was still larger than in 2013 (317,000). So, he could have claimed *this*. Assuming, of course, that the facts were true. But, as it happens, the facts weren't true. He wasn't simply cherry-picking the facts: he was misrepresenting them. The figure in 2017 (for the period between 0000 and 1100) wasn't 420,000: it was 193,000.

This was pointed out to Kellyanne Conway, another spokesperson for Trump. That was when she explained: 'Our press secretary, Sean Spicer, gave alternative facts to that.'

The journalist responded: 'Alternative facts aren't facts. They're falsehoods.'

Later, Conway explained further: 'Two plus two is four. Three plus one is four. Partly cloudy, partly sunny. Glass half full, glass half empty. Those are alternative facts.'[2]

Radical Thinking

Those are, in a sense, alternative facts. Two plus two *is* four. Three plus one *is* four. A glass half full is also a glass half empty. Reality can be described in different ways. However, Spicer's 'alternative facts' weren't true. 193,000 is not also 420,000. It's less than a half-truth, period.

To make sense of any particular claim, you need to begin with the meaning: what's really being claimed. For example, the first claim: *it was the largest audience ever.* You then need to consider the basis of *that* claim: according to DC Metro data (for the relevant time period), this isn't true.

The second claim: *He gave alternative facts.* What does this mean? *Two plus two is four. Three plus one is four. Those are alternative facts.* So, according to *that* meaning, what's the basis for the claim that *he gave alternative facts*? He said that the figure was 420,000 rather than 193,000. That's not true. Two plus two is four. But three plus one isn't seven. That's not an alternative fact. That's an alternative universe.

In the real world, it's tempting to respond with another claim: *Alternative facts are not facts. They're falsehoods.* However, that depends on what you mean. There *are* alternative facts: if you mean 'other' or 'different' facts. If the facts aren't true, of course, then they're falsehoods. But there's a bigger picture beyond the claims and the matter of whether or not they're true. You need to understand the *meaning* of the claim and you need to consider the *basis* of it. However, you also need to consider the *purpose*. The purpose of the first claim was to present Trump as uniquely popular. And, for those who didn't read the fact checks, that would have worked. The purpose of the second claim was to manage the problem with the first claim. And, for those who didn't think it through, that also would have worked.

There are always alternative facts that can be cited. In 2016, Trump won the electoral vote. In 2016, he lost the popular vote. Those are alternative facts. In 2020, Trump lost the electoral vote. In 2020, he lost the popular vote. Those are alternative facts. They're based, in turn, on other facts. They're based on data from polling stations, which most of us assume to be true. But are these facts true? Many have questioned them. They've made claims about widespread fraud. Experts have checked this. They've found no evidence of it. Nevertheless, the claims have persisted.

These sceptics appeal to the facts – but only some of them. They talk about *particular* cases of fraud. And there are always *some* cases of fraud. They claim that, because there were cases of fraud, the election was the result of *widespread* fraud. This a fallacy of ambiguity. Or, perhaps, it's *not* an error: it's a deliberate strategy to exploit ambiguity. It's a conscious attempt to make certain facts relevant, and then to repeat them, over and over again, because this can be persuasive.

These particular facts may or may not be true. However, even if they're true, they don't support the actual claim about widespread fraud. In terms of the bigger picture – not just this election but, say, a different election – we can compare the two and spot the differences. Trump was elected in 2016. He wasn't elected in 2020. Same form, different content. If we assume that the facts are true – in both cases – then he lost in 2020. If we have evidence that the cases are different – for example, that there was widespread fraud in one but not another – then that matters. If we don't, then we've no reason to believe anything else: he lost. Meanwhile, the claims continue because, of course, they're not concerned with the facts. They serve an alternative purpose.

Radical Thinking

Facts are claims that tell us something about the world. They're true, depending on the context, and what they mean, and on the evidence that supports them. If we consider the context, the meaning and the evidence, then we can make sense of them. However, when people make claims and cite facts, we also need to consider their purpose. They'll always present a particular picture. They'll do this for a particular purpose. To inform. To sell. To manipulate.

However, if we consider the context, what they mean, and the basis of their claims, then we can make sense of this too.

It's time for some good news: *Edinburgh is the best city to live in the world*.

This isn't my personal opinion. I'm repeating a claim which was reported in the press. A few years ago, we were told that 'Edinburgh has been named the best city to live in the world.'[3] So, let's have a wee look at that. After all, there's so much fake news going around, you can't be too careful.

The claim was made in a particular context. It was reported in the (Edinburgh) *Evening News*, which is a local newspaper. It wasn't offering a mere local opinion. It explained the meaning and basis of the claim: 'Edinburgh has been named the best city to live in the world thanks to its low crime rate, high levels of education and the overall health of its workforce, according to a new study.'

So far, so good. When they claimed that this is 'the best city to live in the world', they *meant* in terms of 'low crime rate, high levels of education and the overall health of its workforce'. And, when they made this claim, it had a *basis*: it was 'according to a new study'. But that's a tad ambiguous. What study? What, precisely, did it say? We need to look beyond the headlines.

This is what the article in the *Evening News* actually said. It's a useful reminder of how to make sense of the news beyond the headlines:

> The report, published by global consultancy Arcadis, measures the social, environmental and economic health of 100 cities around the globe in its 2018 Sustainability Cities Index. The cities are marked on three pillars of sustainability as set out by Arcadis: people, planet and profit ... The poll sees the Capital top the charts in the people sub-index to claim the title of 'most liveable city in the world' ahead of London, Paris, Singapore and Stockholm. The people category considers the social aspects of living in a city that reflect the overall quality of life of its residents. Indicators include 'education, health, income inequality, work–life balance, crime, demographics and cultural offerings'. The city's lively arts and entertainment culture, the Old and the New Town, both of which are World Heritage Sites, and tourism combine to make it a desirable place to live. ... Edinburgh places third overall behind Stockholm in second place and London in first.

The article ended with a couple of quotes from local councillors. According to one: 'That the data is collected from the perspective of citizens is particularly significant and we will continue to build on our potential so Scotland's cities remain at the forefront in the future.' According to another: 'I can see why Edinburgh has come out top, as it's an amazing city.'

OK, well, that sounds impressive. It's nice to be the 'best' at something.

However, when they claim that this is the 'best city to live in the world', they mean the 'most liveable city in the world'. What does *this* mean? It's based on 'indicators' that include 'education, health, income inequality, work–life balance, crime, demographics and cultural offerings'. So, it's the 'best' – or 'most liveable' – city in the world, according to those indicators. *That* is what they mean.

But what's the basis of *that* claim? It was based on measures of '100 cities around the globe'. There are thousands of cities in the world. So, it's not really the 'best' in 'the world': it's the 'best' of those 100. And where did they get the data? It was based on a 'poll' and 'the data is collected from the perspective of citizens'. So, it's the 'best' of those 100 cities – according to citizens of those cities. Still, in *that* sense and on *that* basis, it's the 'best'.

However, there was a bigger picture. The poll was based on 'three pillars of sustainability: people, planet and profit'. And Edinburgh was top of the 'people' charts. It wasn't the top overall. As you may have spotted: 'Edinburgh places third overall behind Stockholm in second place and London in first.' So, according to the overall study, it was actually London that claimed top spot.

Why didn't they just tell us *that*? That, of course, is a matter of context (looking farther – at how the study was reported in other contexts – the headline was that London came out top). When we consider the context of the claim about Edinburgh being the 'best' city in the world, the purpose of telling us *this* is clear. The *Evening News* is a local paper. For local people. Its purpose is to inform its readers by reporting what's locally relevant. There's also a practical purpose: to sell newspapers. They do this by reporting stories from a local perspective, so that locals find them appealing.

You can make sense of anything

So, it wasn't fake news. It presented a particular picture, based on relevant facts. Nevertheless, it was a few years ago. Since then, other polls have come to different conclusions, based on different data. In one of them, Edinburgh didn't make it into the top ten cities to live in the world. This, of course, wasn't good news. However, whether or not it's good news depends on the actual claim. After all, a glass half empty is also a glass half full.

When the *Evening News* reported this poll, it announced: 'A study has named Edinburgh as one of the best cities to live in the UK.'[4]

The meaning of a claim isn't always obvious. Sometimes its *meaning* is tied to its *basis*. Sometimes its *meaning* is tied to its *purpose*. To think critically about knowledge claims, we need to consider all three in context.

In April 1988, for example, a newspaper published the headline: 'World War 2 Bomber Found on Moon'.[5]

The context was the front page of the *Sunday Sport*, a weekly newspaper that would go on to publish other remarkable headlines, such as 'Donkey Robs Bank' and 'Adolf Hitler Was a Woman'. Its pages were dominated by sensationalist stories, in large font and short sentences, and by pictures of scantily clad young women. Nevertheless, it described itself as a 'newspaper': literally, as 'The People's Newspaper'. For some people, it was *their* newspaper. At the time, I knew people who bought it every week, and they didn't buy another Sunday paper. And, in April 1988, one of them showed me his copy. As he did, he explained that a 'World War 2 bomber' had 'apparently' been found on the moon. That was how I heard the news.

What was the meaning of this claim? That depends on the *actual* claim. The claim made by the newspaper was: 'World War 2 Bomber

Found on Moon'. The claim made by my colleague was that this was 'apparently' true. That's a thing that people do: they present a claim in a particular way by adding some words that make it clear that the source of the claim is somewhere else. This changes the meaning of the claim.

They may tie the meaning to the *basis* of the claim. For example: '*According to a study*, Edinburgh is the best city to live in the world.' That's not the same as the direct claim: 'Edinburgh is the best city to live in the world.' And, if they tell us *which* study, then we can check the basis of the claim. However, they might do it in an ambiguous way. For example, '*I read somewhere that* a World War 2 bomber was found on the moon.' If they don't provide the actual source, then we don't know the *basis* of the claim.

Nevertheless, doing this serves a *purpose*: it distances the claim from the person making it. It allows them to repeat the claim without being accountable for the claim itself. They're only accountable for what *they* claim: for example, that they 'read it somewhere'. This makes what *they* say harder to challenge. It may be true that they 'read it somewhere', but what matters is if what 'they read' is true. To make sense of that, we need to know *where* they read it: so that we can check its basis.

In this case, it was obvious where my colleague had read it. When he said 'apparently', he meant according to the *Sunday Sport*. The basis of the *Sunday Sport* claim, however, was far from clear. It was accompanied by a suspiciously hazy picture of a B52 on rocky ground that, in this context, was supposed to be interpreted as the moon's surface. It presented the claim in a particular way – '*It is claimed* the shock pictures have been sent to world leaders', 'President Reagan *is said to be* perplexed and gravely concerned over the puzzling pictures', 'The Soviets *are reported to be* ...', and so on. It didn't specify who *claimed*, who *said* or who *reported* anything. In short, they gave no basis for the claim.

However, the meaning of the claim was still not clear: it was also tied to its *purpose*. This was the first time that I'd seen the *Sunday Sport*, and I didn't know if it was meant to be taken seriously. I didn't know if its readers took it seriously. If the purpose was to inform, then that meant one thing. If the purpose was to amuse, then that meant something else. In hindsight, of course, the purpose of the claim wasn't to inform: it was to sell. Flamboyant headlines attract attention. When something sounds extraordinary, you tend to be more curious about what to believe. So, people bought the newspaper. They may or may not have believed what they read. They may have simply thought that it was an amusing story to share.

Nevertheless, these claims have an influence: they direct our attention to this not that. In April 1988, on the same day that the *Sunday Sport* reported that a 'World War 2 Bomber' had been found on the moon, the front page of the *Observer* newspaper reported the following: a car bomb attack in Lebanon; the Duke of Edinburgh's views about apartheid; the level of public support for the government (as they were cutting benefits and introducing the poll tax); and the increased use of television adverts, paid for by the taxpayer, to promote government policies. It also included references to the shooting of a protester on the West Bank, the arrest of peace protesters in Britain, and the 'rising tide of racism and Fascism in Britain and Europe'.[6] Meanwhile, the front page of the *Sunday Sport* promised to 'expose the evils behind lust-crazed devil-worshippers' and to reveal 'Britain's biggest glamour model!' It promised bigger pictures. However, even for its more sceptical readers, it didn't provide the bigger picture. It provided an amusing diversion.

Since then, flamboyant claims have continued, and they've continued to divert attention from the bigger picture. The purpose of some has been to sell newspapers. The purpose of others has been to manipulate how we think. For example, in 1994, *The Sun* newspaper claimed that the European Union had 'outlaw[ed] curved bananas'.[7] This wasn't true. It was the sort of thing that Boris Johnson said – at that time, he was already well known for making up silly claims about the EU. In 2016, during the Brexit campaign, Johnson was still talking bananas. 'It is absurd that we are told that you cannot sell bananas in bunches of more than two or three.'[8] It *was* absurd. It wasn't true. However, if anyone believed that it *was* true, then they might think this sort of bureaucratic nonsense was a good reason why Britain should 'take back control'.

There's nothing new about fake news. People continue to peddle it because it serves a purpose. It can get us to think about this not that. It can make us wonder if, *perhaps*, it's true. It allows people to repeat the claim in a way that avoids accountability: they have merely read or heard it somewhere. When it's repeated enough, however, people assume that there must be something to it. And, later, when it's shown to be a falsehood, they never admit that they lied. They pretend that they didn't really mean *that*. They pretend that they weren't being *serious*. They then continue to make further claims in the hope that nobody remembers that the original claim had no basis in evidence.

In August 1988, four months after the original headline, the *Sunday Sport* declared: 'World War 2 Bomber Found on Moon Vanishes'.[9]

'You can make sense of anything.'

This claim was made in a particular context: it was the title of this chapter.

What does it mean? 'You' means the reader, and 'can' means that you're *able* to do so, not that you necessarily *will*. In other words, you need to do it. To 'make sense of anything' means to understand any claim that you encounter, no matter how extraordinary it might seem. It may be presented as a fact. It may be presented as something that's based on facts.

However, it's one of our habits to draw a boundary between facts and interpretation. This assumes that facts are true. In principle, this makes sense. In practice, however, we can't be certain if any particular 'fact' is true. A fact might be based on numbers and, some would say, numbers don't lie. That's true. Numbers can't speak. So, like facts, they can't speak for themselves. That's why people need to collect numbers and then present them as facts. When they do, these numbers are accompanied by words, which have particular meanings. This requires interpretation.

For example, four is a number and four per cent is a percentage. 'Unemployment is four per cent' is a fact. In other words, it's true. Here and now. If the numbers are reliable. However, the numbers that we get depend on how we define 'unemployment'. This can mean different things to different people, so it can be measured in different ways. There are people in permanent and temporary jobs, in full-time jobs and part-time jobs, many of which have zero-hour contracts. The facts may be true, but they're based on a particular meaning of 'unemployment'. Facts, with or without numbers, still need to be interpreted, so that we know what they mean.

Radical Thinking

The basis of the claim 'You can make sense of anything' (meaning: any claim that you encounter, no matter how extraordinary it might seem) is logic and evidence. The logic is this:

If you're reading this book, then you can make sense of it.

You've read about claims ranging from the most ordinary (for example, 'It's raining') to the most extraordinary (for example, 'World War 2 Bomber Found on Moon').

Therefore, you can (probably) make sense of anything.

It's not certain. This isn't a *valid* argument: it doesn't *necessarily* follow. It's an inference based on evidence. The evidence is that you've read this far and that, having studied extraordinary beliefs for years, I can tell you that other claims are no harder to understand than the ones included here.[10] All claims take a similar form: something is (or isn't) the case. What, precisely, is the case depends on what they mean. So, when we understand *what* they mean, we can then consider the basis of *that* claim.

This may seem obvious. However, it's not. We're surrounded by claims about this versus that, and much of the confusion is the result of people arguing about different things. In recent years, as we argued about Brexit, we were arguing about different things. We were told that 'Brexit means Brexit', but we didn't know what *that* meant. People drew particular boundaries between 'hard' and 'soft', 'deal' or 'no deal'. We were told that a deal was 'oven-ready'. Then we were told, in different headlines, that 'Boris got Brexit done'. Years later, as he was being forced to resign for making less-than-a-half-truth statements, he was still redrawing the boundaries of the deal (the one that was meant to be done). Clearly, whatever you think about Brexit, and whatever we thought we were arguing about, we weren't arguing about the same thing.

Facts may be true, but the facts that we encounter are always particular facts, which present a particular picture of reality. They're based on drawing particular boundaries: between 'unemployment' and 'employment', or between Brexit being done and not being done. The purpose of reporting particular facts might be to inform, or to sell, or to manipulate. It might be to get you to buy into this, or to get you to change your mind about that. 'Under this government, unemployment has fallen.' 'Since Brexit, inflation has risen.' The facts may be true, but they *imply* something else: that the government deserves credit, or that Brexit is responsible. As we saw in Chapter 10, when particular facts are described in particular ways, this can suggest responsibility.

Whatever the claim, it has a context. If we consider the meaning of the claim, its basis and its purpose, then we can make sense of it. The extraordinary claims of conspiracy theorists are no harder to understand. But there are *particular* claims. The election was rigged. The earth is flat. The US government was responsible for 9/11. All of these claims have a context. Elections might be swayed in various ways. It once seemed obvious that the earth was flat. If I say that the US government was responsible for 9/11, however, the context is obvious.

So, let's start with the meaning. What's the actual claim? After all, when people claim that the US government was responsible for 9/11, they mean different things. Some claim that the government knew in advance and failed to prevent the attacks. Some claim that the government actually planned and carried out the attacks.[11] But let's consider a common theme: the US government is hiding the truth about their role in the 9/11 attacks.

Now, what's the basis of this claim? When the claim is that evidence is being hidden, you can't expect too much in terms of evidence.

Radical Thinking

However, conspiracy theorists cite pieces of evidence that apparently contradict the official story, and point to evidence of other government cover-ups (such as Watergate, or the Iran–Contra affair, or the lack of evidence of 'weapons of mass destruction' in Iraq).[12]

In the process, conspiracy theorists do their best to sound persuasive (as discussed in Chapter 6). They present themselves as honest and competent (they seek the truth, and *they* were able to discover errors in the official story). They present these beliefs as plausible (the government has done this sort of thing before). They present what they say as relevant and appealing (they're asking *important* questions and, surely, everyone *wants* to know the truth).

What's the purpose of the claim? It might be to inform. After all, they may be sincere and, since we can't be certain, they *may* be right. It might be to sell. Conspiracy theorists can profit from websites and podcasts and books. And, of course, it might be to manipulate. The recent surge in conspiracy theories has been part and parcel of recent practices in political propaganda. Or, perhaps, the purpose is personal. It could be an attempt to find kindred spirits, or to be seen by others as a defender of Truth. For some who voice these opinions, it may be how they cope with a messy and uncertain world.

There are many ways to make sense of these claims. But I know what you're thinking: what about the truth? The *actual* truth? That, of course, will depend on the *actual* claim. If the US government is hiding the truth about 9/11, then what, *precisely*, are they hiding? After all, there's bound to be some security information that they've not revealed. That's not necessarily a 'cover-up'. If they knew in advance about the attacks, then what, *precisely*, did they know? After all, they must have known that something like this might happen at some point. That's not the same as knowing that *this* would happen on 11 September 2001. Once we know the actual claim, we can consider the supporting evidence. Like any claim, before we can make sense of it, we need to know what we're *actually* talking about. Like any claim, it will depend on the reliability of the evidence that supports it.

Nothing is certain. Anything is possible. The government may be hiding the truth. There's certainly evidence of previous government cover-ups. However, there's a bigger picture: the previous government cover-ups were exposed by the mainstream media. The most powerful country in the world was unable to prevent the truth from coming out. That might be interpreted as evidence of their limits. There may, of course, be other cover-ups. And, in time, the truth may out. Until then, we can make sense of what (to us, here and now) are the most extraordinary claims, and we can understand why people might make such claims.

The purpose of the claim 'You can make sense of anything' is to remind you that you can do it. However, you need to remember your limits. You don't see the world like a camera. Your mind isn't simply a computer. You're prone to illogical and unscientific thinking. You're human. But non-human things have their limits too. Cameras and computers can record and compute. However, they can't *understand*. They can't *make sense* of things. That's what humans do. It's something that *only* we can do. We're neither cameras nor computers. We may be prone to illogical and unscientific thinking. However, we invented cameras and computers, logic and science. So, we can understand their limits. And we can understand each other. If we listen.

We have no access to absolute truth. We can't be truly objective because we see things from our current position. However, we can understand different perspectives. We can think about what we're missing. We can consider alternative views, see what they mean, look at the evidence, and think about why they're telling us this. We don't *need* to agree with them. We need only accept what this makes obvious. Nothing is certain, but we can make sense of anything.

And without uncertainty, where would we be?

We'd be in a world without curiosity.

EXIT:
BEYOND THE SQUARE

It's time to leave George Square. That's ~~what I think~~ the conclusion that I've reached for the moment. No doubt I'll return here later. Well, not *no* doubt. Nothing is certain.

I'm walking in the direction of Salisbury Crags. I'm passing by several windows. Through them, I see glimpses of staff and students. I'm assuming that they're 'staff' or 'students'. They might be other kinds of folk. I can't see who they really are.

I'm on West Nicolson Street, passing windows to restaurants and cafés, to a tattoo studio and a hairdresser. They're displaying their wares in particular ways – in menus with appealing descriptions, or in photographs of attractive young people – to encourage consumption or a change in appearance.

I'm now at a crossroads. The traffic is busy, but nobody is actually going anywhere. Everyone is waiting for the lights to change. A driver is leaning forward in his seat, eager to get to his destination. From his view through his windscreen, everyone else appears to be in his way. Meanwhile, a pedestrian is pressing the crossing button, over and over again, trying to persuade the lights that her destination is more important.

Radical Thinking

As we wait impatiently, for a matter of seconds, I can hear a snippet of conversation: 'Yeah, that *really* pisses me off.' However, without the wider context, I can't understand what it means. Then the context becomes obvious, when I notice that a cyclist is breaking the rules. The pissed-off pedestrian yells at the passing cyclist, who immediately yells back at him, though neither can hear what the other is saying as the distance between them increases.

The pedestrians cross, though not until we get permission from the pedestrian crossing, and not without checking for another cyclist, since we're now aware that not everyone plays by the same rules as we do. I'm heading down West Richmond Street, between a discount supermarket and a pawnbroker, whose windows promise different kinds of bargains, which always come at a cost to others.

The view of Salisbury Crags, as you cross the Pleasance. The Radical Road, which climbs from left to right, is currently empty.

Exit: Beyond the square

Beyond the competitive bustle of the main road, where individuals are trying to avoid each other, or to get in front of each other, the path is slower and calmer. I'm now crossing the Pleasance. As I do, I can see Salisbury Crags in front of me.

I'm wandering down Brown Street, and turning into a square garden. It's called Bauks View. Two centuries ago, it was called Salisbury Square. It was a modest square, where tenement neighbours who made their livings – as builders, or butchers, or booksellers – might chat about their various trades, and where Mrs Profit, who offered humble lodgings, could dry the clothes of her guests.[1] Today, it's an uncultivated piece of land (a bauk), where a diverse range of plants can grow, exotic urban wildlife can visit, and people can come to sit on benches to take in the grand view of Salisbury Crags. They changed the name because it's no longer about the square: it's about the larger view.

I'm continuing down the street, and now I find myself at another crossroads. However, it's not for drivers or pedestrians, because it's not really about getting, whether by car or by foot, to a destination. It's for people taking a walk. No person is just one thing – drivers are also pedestrians, and pedestrians are walkers – but this is a path that makes the process, rather than the outcome, relevant.

The main path goes to the left and to the right. The less obvious path is directly ahead. It's a rockier path, and a little slippery, but the gradient isn't particularly steep. It bends to the right, then to the left, and then there are stairs that lead up to another level. From here, there are more paths, and people take different ones. And, as they pass others, who are going in a different direction, they smile and greet them. There are no windows here. There are no advertisements. There are various options and time to consider them. I've chosen a path, though I might have picked a different one, but I can see that, if I go farther up this one, there's an opening in the trees.

From this position, I can see Salisbury Crags. The Radical Road is right in front of me. It's still out of bounds — the authorities continue to be concerned about falling rocks — though I see no falling rocks. At the top of the Crags, there's someone looking down at the Road, wondering why it's deserted. At the foot of the Crags, there's someone looking up at the only route that seems to be available, which is steeper. They're wondering if they'll be able to make it.

The Radical Road is visible, but it's not for looking at. You need to walk it. It's not as steep as the alternatives. You don't need to focus so much attention on getting to where you want to go. This gives you time to look around, and to appreciate different views. It gives you time to engage with people who are heading in a different direction.

Behind me, there's a cul-de-sac, where residents have a view of the Crags. If you live there, you can see the Radical Road through your own window. The view must be satisfying, but it's fixed. It might change in appearance, from season to season, but the basic content remains the same, and it's always seen from the same angle. If you want to see more, you won't see it through the window. You need to leave the comfort of your own space. You need to walk beyond the cul-de-sac.

If you walk farther, then you see different things, and you see them from different angles. You notice things that you hadn't noticed before. You look at the world in a different way. You encounter others who see things differently, because their views are also limited, but what they offer is an alternative perspective. You can simply pass them by, or you can stop for a moment to see where they're coming from. You don't need to follow them. You can continue on your way. However, you get a better sense of the territory. You have a greater appreciation of where you are, where you're going, and where else you might be.

As I look ahead, I'm interrupted by an elderly local who says, 'Good morning.' Yes, it's a fine day. Then a Labrador walks up and sniffs my hand. He's curious and in search of human contact. I tickle him behind the ears as I chat with his owner about how dogs, who don't worry about what people think, give us permission to talk to strangers. A tourist approaches and asks if one of us – she seems to think that we're friends – would mind taking a photograph of her and her family in front of this beautiful landscape.

She asks about the best places to go, and about how best to get there. We provide competing advice, and different directions, but that's not a problem. There are many places to go, and various ways to get there. People have their preferences. It doesn't have to be about getting it right. And, since you're not here for long, your experience is bound to be limited, so you'll never know if you got it right.

For the brief time that you're here, however, you can discover things that are new to you, and find them curious. You can appreciate the differences. That way, before you go, you have a better sense of the bigger picture.

ACKNOWLEDGEMENTS

This began as a new kind of university course on critical thinking, which was halted by a global pandemic. So, it went in a different direction. It wouldn't have got much farther if not for my brilliant agent (Jaime Marshall), who found a way to move forward, until it caught up with Swift Press, where my publisher (Mark Richards) and my editor (Jack Ramm) then helped to take it farther. My copy-editor (Ian Howe) helped to cover up my errers, and my production team (Tetragon) turned it into a book. Along the way, there were local guides who gave directions at specific points (Dr Claudia Coelho, Dr Alex Doumas, Prof. Michael Gill, Dr Sandra Marwick and Prof. Richard Wiseman) and local places run by local people (Edinburgh University Library and the National Library of Scotland), who made progress possible. All of them helped along the way, but none of them should be held accountable for where it ended up. Wherever that might be …

NOTES

DEDICATION

1   This is a note for the genuinely curious. Naturally, most readers won't check this. But *you* did, which tells me that you're my *real* audience. So, for what it's worth, here's what it means: it's a personal thing. When I completed my PhD, many years ago, I wrote the dedication: *To my parents, who will never read it*. After all, nobody reads doctoral theses. When I completed my first popular book, I wrote the dedication: *To my parents, who never read my doctoral thesis*. It was a wee in-joke, which nobody was supposed to get. However, a few years ago, I told my parents about it, and they found it amusing. Then my dad died in 2019, before I started writing this book, and then my mum died in 2022, before I finished it. So, they won't read this either. However, they would have found it amusing.

WHERE TO START?

1   This is a wee homage to a local alliterative rhyme that we learned as children: 'Round and round the Radical Road, the radical rascal ran ...'
2   The road has been closed since 2018 due to falling rocks.

3   Lamont, P. (2020). 'The construction of critical thinking: between how we think and what we believe', *History of Psychology*, 23(3), 232–51, p. 233.
4   Ibid.

1. WHAT WE NOTICE

1   Doyle, A. C. (1892). *The Adventures of Sherlock Holmes*. New York: Harper & Brothers, p. 6.
2   Leary, D. E. (1994). *Metaphors in the History of Psychology*. Cambridge: Cambridge University Press.
3   Mackaill, A. and Kemp, D. (2007). *Conan Doyle and Joseph Bell: The Real Sherlock Holmes*. Edinburgh: Royal College Surgeons of Edinburgh, p. 47.
4   Doyle, A. C. (1924). *Memories and Adventures*. London: Hodder & Stoughton, p. 26.
5   Mackaill and Kemp, *Conan Doyle and Joseph Bell*, p. 52.
6   Liebow, E. (1982). *Dr. Joe Bell: Model for Sherlock Holmes*. Bowling Green, Ohio: Bowling Green University Popular Press, p. 10.
7   Mackaill and Kemp, *Conan Doyle and Joseph Bell*, p. 52.
8   Doyle, A. C. (1930). *The Edge of the Unknown*. London: John Murray.
9   Houdini, H. (1972). *A Magician Among the Spirits*. New York: Arno Press, p. 161.
10 Doyle, *Edge of the Unknown*, Chapter 1; Houdini, *A Magician Among the Spirits*.
11 'Empire Palace Theatre', *The Scotsman*, 7 April 1914, p. 4.
12 Lamont, P. (2016). 'Modern magic, the illusion of transformation, and how it was done', *Journal of Social History*, 55(4), 854–74, https://doi.org/10.1093/jsh/shw126.
13 Robert-Houdin, J.-E. (1878). *The Secrets of Conjuring and Magic; or, How to Become a Wizard, Translated and Edited by Professor Hoffmann*. London: George Routledge and Sons, p. 35.

14 Ibid., pp. 33–4.
15 The most popular was Hoffmann, L. (1876). *Modern Magic: A Practical Treatise on the Art of Conjuring*. London: George Routledge and Sons.
16 Houdini, *A Magician Among the Spirits*.
17 Ibid., p. 164.
18 Lamont, P. (2006). 'Magician as conjuror: a frame analysis of Victorian mediums', *Early Popular Visual Culture*, 4(1), 131–42.
19 Simons, D. J. and Chabris, C. F. (1999). 'Gorillas in our midst: sustained inattentional blindness for dynamic events', *Perception*, 28(9), 1059–74.
20 Rubio, A. (2019). 'Christ on the comal', *Eater*, 23 April. https://www.eater.com/2019/4/23/18412505/jesus-tortilla-original-maria-rubio-new-mexico.
21 Allen, W. (1983). *Without Feathers*. New York: Ballantine Books, p. 193.

2. A LIMITED PICTURE

1 These were, respectively, Andrew Bell and Colin Macfarquhar (Kafker, F. (1995). 'The achievement of Andrew Bell and Colin Macfarquhar as the first publishers of the *Encyclopaedia Britannica*', *British Journal for Eighteenth-Century Studies*, 18(2), 139–52).
2 *Encyclopaedia Britannica* (eleventh edition), p. vii. This referred explicitly to the second edition, which is the edition being discussed in this chapter.
3 The first edition of *Encyclopaedia Britannica* was printed in Macfarquhar's printing house on Nicolson Street. The second edition was printed just around the corner, just off Richmond Street (Kafker, 'The achievement of Andrew Bell and Colin MacFarquhar', pp. 140–2).
4 Kafker, 'The achievement of Andrew Bell and Colin MacFarquhar', p. 141.

5   *Encyclopaedia Britannica* (second edition), title page.
6   Barnes, H. E. (1917). 'Sociology before Comte: a summary of doctrines and an introduction to the literature', *American Journal of Sociology*, 23(2), p. 234.
7   Lockhart, J. G. (1828). *Life of Robert Burns*. Edinburgh: Constable and Co., p. 151. The meeting was famously depicted in a painting by Charles Martin Hardie, which now hangs in the Dunedin Public Art Gallery in New Zealand.
8   *Encyclopaedia Britannica* (second edition), p. 3649.
9   Ibid., p. 3650.
10 Ibid., p.3680.
11 Kafker, 'The achievement of Andrew Bell and Colin MacFarquhar', p. 143.
12 *Encyclopaedia Britannica* (second edition), p. iii.
13 Ibid., p. vii.
14 Ibid., p. 4068.
15 Ibid., p. 8965.
16 This is according to a recent UNICEF report (Castres, P., Chahal, K. and Sollis, L. (2020). *Ending Preventable Child Deaths: How Britain Can Lead the Way*. London: UNICEF UK, p. 11).
17 Hutton, J. (1788). *The Theory of the Earth: From the Transactions of the Royal Society of Edinburgh*. Edinburgh: Royal Society of Edinburgh, p. 96.
18 Young, R. M. (1985). *Darwin's Metaphor: Nature's Place in Victorian Culture*. Cambridge: Cambridge University Press, p. 84.
19 The argument was a simplified version of a thesis proposed by P. H. Gosse. Gosse, P. H. (1857). *Omphalos: An Attempt to Untie the Geological Knot*. London: John van Voorst.
20 This argument was made by Bertrand Russell: 'There is no logical impossibility in the hypothesis that the world sprang into being five minutes ago.' Russell, B. (1921). *The Analysis of Mind*. London: George Allen & Unwin, p. 159.
21 This is based on Carl Sagan's 'Cosmic Calendar', a concept for

visualising the chronology of the universe that was popularised by Sagan in his 1977 book *Dragons of Eden* and on his 1980 television series *Cosmos*.

22 Playfair, J. (1802). *Illustrations of the Huttonian Theory of the Earth*. London: Cadell and Davies, p. 14.

3. HOW WE INTERPRET THINGS

1 Tait, M. and Forbes Gray, W. (1948). 'George Square: Annals of an Edinburgh locality, 1766–1926, from authentic records', *The Book of the Old Edinburgh Club. Twenty-sixth Volume*. Edinburgh: T. and A. Constable, p. 83.

2 Ibid.

3 Edinburgh Post directories changed the name between the 1805–6 and 1806–7 editions.

4 https://www.ed.ac.uk/news/students/2020/equality-diversity-and-inclusion-an-update.

5 For a fascinating discussion of this issue, by experts on Hume, see 'Edinburgh Philosophy – Voices on Hume', https://blogs.ed.ac.uk/davidhumetower-philosophy/.

6 Lownie, R. (2020). 'When it comes to slavery, 40 George Square should worry us more than DHT', *The Student*, 27 October.

7 St George's Square was renamed Charlotte Square (after Queen Charlotte, the queen at the time).

8 Boswell, J. (1785). *The Journal of a Tour to the Hebrides with Samuel Johnson*. London: Charles Dilly, p. 13.

9 Munnery, S. (2007). *Hello* [DVD]. Go Faster Stripe/Simon Munnery.

10 At the very least, you just thought of both.

11 Potter, J. (1996). *Representing Reality: Discourse, Rhetoric and Social Construction*. London: Sage, p. 132ff.

4. OUR POINTS OF VIEW

1   Doyle, A. C. (1926). *The History of Spiritualism*. London: Cassell & Co., pp. 250–73.
2   Houdini, H. (1972). *A Magician Among the Spirits*. New York: Arno Press, pp. 17–37.
3   'The brothers Davenport in Edinburgh', *The Scotsman*, 3 March 1866, p. 7.
4   Daniel Dennett distinguishes between implicit and explicit beliefs, calling the latter 'opinions': Dennett, D. (1991). 'Two contrasts: folk craft versus folk science, and belief versus opinion,' in J. D. Greenwood, ed., *The Future of Folk Psychology: Intentionality and Cognitive Science*. Cambridge: Cambridge University Press, pp. 135–48.
5   'The Davenport brothers in Liverpool', *Morning Post*, 16 February 1865, p. 3.
6   Lamont, P. (2013). *Extraordinary Beliefs: A Historical Approach to a Psychological Problem*. Cambridge: Cambridge University Press, p. 147.
7   Ibid., p. 161.
8   This point was made regarding several mediums, including the Davenports (ibid., pp. 160–2).
9   Ibid., p. 162.
10 This was, in effect, the 'white crow' argument of William James.
11 Lamont, *Extraordinary Beliefs*, p. 160.
12 Billig, M. (1987). *Arguing and Thinking: A Rhetorical Approach to Social Psychology*. Cambridge: Cambridge University Press.
13 Lamont, *Extraordinary Beliefs*, p. 181ff.
14 Lamont, P. (2004). 'Spiritualism and a mid-Victorian crisis of evidence', *Historical Journal*, 47(4), 897–920.

5. LOCAL CUSTOMS AND HABITS

1   It's not the first time that Hume has been the object of misrepresentation. The street on which the famous atheist lived was given the name St David's Street.

2   Sagan made the comment on his TV show, *Cosmos*, though others had made the point already, including Marcello Truzzi in 1978 (Truzzi M. (1978). 'On the extraordinary: an attempt at clarification', *Zetetic Scholar*, 1(1), p. 11).

3   Hume, D. (1760). *Essays and Treatises on Several Subjects. In Four Volumes. Vol. 1.* London: A. Millar, p. 337.

4   Ibid., p. 337.

5   Kemp Smith, N., ed. (1948). *Hume's Dialogues Concerning Natural Religion.* 2nd edition. New York: Social Sciences Publishers, p. 77.

6   Hunter, M. (1992). '"Aikenhead the Atheist": The context and consequences of articulate irreligion in the late seventeenth century', in M. Hunter and D. Wootton, eds, *Atheism from the Reformation to the Enlightenment.* Oxford: Oxford University Press, p. 237.

7   He argued for 'gradual' abolition. The reasons for this are disputed (e.g. Mullen, S. (2021). 'Henry Dundas: a "great delayer" of the abolition of the Atlantic slave trade', *Scottish Historical Review*, 100(2), 218–48; McCarthy, A. (2023). 'Henry Dundas and the abolition of the British slave trade: further evidence', *Scottish Affairs*, 32(3), 334–46), but this is why his statue in central Edinburgh currently has a plaque stating that he 'was instrumental in delaying the abolition of slavery'.

8   Whyte, I. (2006). *Scotland and the Abolition of Black Slavery, 1756–1838.* Edinburgh: Edinburgh University Press, p. 42.

9   Whyte, I. (2012). *Send Back the Money! The Free Church of Scotland and American Slavery.* Edinburgh: James Clarke.

10   Whyte, *Scotland and the Abolition of Black Slavery*, p. 57.

11   Thorndike, E. (1920). 'A constant error in psychological ratings', *Journal of Applied Psychology*, 4(1), 25–9.

12   Ross, L. (1977). 'The intuitive psychologist and his shortcomings:

distortions in the attribution process', in L. Berkowitz, ed., *Advances in Experimental Social Psychology* (vol. 10, pp. 173–220). New York: Academic Press, p. 187.

13 Bondeson, J. (2011). *Greyfriars Bobby: The Most Faithful Dog in the World.* Stroud: Amberley Publishing.

14 Algeo, M. (2015). *Abe and Fido: Lincoln's Love of Animals and the Touching Story of his Favorite Canine Companion.* Chicago: Chicago Review Press.

15 This is a rather simplistic take on a (naturally) more complicated development, discussed by the historian E. P. Thompson (Thompson, E. P. (1967). 'Time and work-discipline in industrial capitalism', *Past and Present*, 38(1), 56–97), which others since have revised (e.g. Birth, K. (2022). 'Capital flows, itinerant laborers, and time: a revision of Thompson's thesis of time and work discipline', *Time and Society*, 31(3), 392–414).

16 https://www.edinburghnews.scotsman.com/news/campaign-launched-salute-edinburghs-greatest-women-600927.

17 For a long list of options, see Sheridan, S. (2019). *Where Are the Women? A Guide to an Imagined Scotland.* Edinburgh: Historic Environment Scotland, pp. 11–39.

18 See also https://www.edinburghnews.scotsman.com/news/opinion/columnists/its-time-to-celebrate-achievements-of-citys-women-susan-dalgety-3554837.

19 For a sympathetic take on Stopes' eugenicist views, see Debenham, C. (2018). 'Marie Stopes as a maverick eugenicist', in *Marie Stopes' Sexual Revolution and the Birth Control Movement.* Basingstoke: Palgrave Macmillan, pp. 121–31.

6. TOOLS OF PERSUASION

1 Bennett, J. H. (1851). *The Mesmeric Mania of 1851, with a Physiological Explanation of the Phenomena Produced.* Edinburgh: Sutherland and Knox, pp. 5–6.

2   Ibid., p. 6.
3   Ibid., p. 5.
4   Ibid., p. 11.
5   Winter, A. (1997). *Mesmerized: Powers of Mind in Victorian Britain*. Chicago: University of Chicago Press, p. 226.
6   Lamont, P. (2020). 'Hypnosis and suggestion: a historical perspective', in O. Braddick, ed., *Oxford Research Encyclopedia of Psychology*. Oxford: Oxford University Press.
7   According to him, they were 'ignorant and mercenary' (Bennett, *Mesmeric Mania*, p. 20).
8   Ibid., p. 14.
9   According to him, it was an 'unphysiological doctrine' (ibid., p. 21), and it 'may be injurious' (ibid., p. 20).
10 Ibid., p. 20.
11 Gregory, W. (1851). *Letters to a Candid Inquirer, on Animal Magnetism*. London: Taylor, Walton and Maberly, p. 2.
12 Ibid., p. 11.
13 Ibid., pp. viii, 7, 40.
14 Lamont, P. (2013) *Extraordinary Beliefs: A Historical Approach to a Psychological Problem*. Cambridge: Cambridge University Press, p. 63ff.
15 Scott, W. D. (1912). 'Suggestion', *Psychological Bulletin*, 9(7), 269–71.
16 Hollingworth, H. (1913). *Advertising and Selling: Principles of Appeal and Response*. New York: D. Appleton and Company.
17 Sproule, J. M. (1997). *Propaganda and Democracy: The American Experience of Media and Mass Persuasion*. Cambridge: Cambridge University Press.
18 Institute for Propaganda Analysis (1937), 'How to Detect Propaganda', *Propaganda Analysis*, 1(2), 5–8, p. 5.
19 Congressional Record: Proceedings and Debates of the 76th Congress, Third Session, 86 (11), Washington: United States Government Printing Office, 1941, p. 12392.
20 'How to Detect Propaganda', p. 7.

Radical Thinking

21 Ibid.
22 Ibid., p. 5.
23 Watson, G. and Glaser, E. (1942). *Watson–Glaser Tests of Critical Thinking. Battery II: Logical Reasoning.* New York: World Book Company, p. 10.
24 You're clearly a curious person. Or impatient? Fair enough. If we assume that 'No radicals are patriotic people' and that 'All patriotic people are to be admired', then this is like saying 'No dogs are cats' and that 'All cats should be admired'. But there *might* be some dogs who should be admired. If we assume the initial statements, then we cannot conclude that no dogs, or that all dogs, or that some dogs should be admired. But this is a possibility. So none of these conclusions *necessarily* follows.
25 Lamont, P. (2020). 'The construction of "critical thinking": between how we think and what we believe', *History of Psychology*, 23(3), 232–51, p. 240.
26 For example, John Baird, one of the leaders of the Radical War of 1820, had fought in the British army.
27 Cialdini, R. (1984). *Influence: The Psychology of Persuasion.* New York: HarperCollins. The original book presented six principles. More recently, a seventh has been added (Cialdini, R. (2007). *Influence, New and Expanded: The Psychology of Persuasion.* New York: HarperCollins.
28 The latter is the recent seventh principle: Cialdini (2007), *Influence*.
29 Hitler, A. (1971). *Mein Kampf.* Translated by Ralph Manheim. Boston: Houghton Mifflin, p. 179ff.
30 Kahneman, D. (2011). *Thinking, Fast and Slow.* New York: Farrar, Strauss and Giroux.

7. HOW WE FEEL

1 Leary, D. E. (1994). *Metaphors in the History of Psychology.* Cambridge: Cambridge University Press, p. 107.

2 *An Act for Opening an Easy and Commodious Communication from the High Street of Edinburgh to the Country Southward*, 1785, I, p. 2.
3 Dixon, T. (2003). *From Passions to Emotions: The Creation of a Secular Psychological Category*. Cambridge: Cambridge University Press.
4 Brown, T. (1820). *Lectures on the Philosophy of the Human Mind*, Vol. I. Edinburgh: W. and C. Tait.
5 Ortony, A. and Turner, T. (1990). 'What's basic about basic emotions?', *Psychological Review*, 97(3), 315–31.
6 This was based on the assumption that emotions were either positive or negative, and that surprise and interest were neutral, though others questioned that assumption (ibid., p. 317).
7 Harré, R. and Gillet, G. (1994). *The Discursive Mind*. London: Sage, p. 147.
8 LaMothe, R. (2007). 'An analysis of acedia', *Pastoral Psychology*, 56(1), 15–30.
9 The next few paragraphs are based on Lamont, P. (2017), 'A particular kind of wonder: the experience of magic past and present', *Review of General Psychology*, 21(1), 1–8.
10 Ibid., p. 1.
11 Stearns, P. and Knapp, M. (1996). 'Historical perspectives on grief', in R. Harré and W. G. Parrott, eds, *The Emotions: Social, Cultural and Biological Dimensions*. London: Sage.
12 Ronson, J. (2015). *So You've Been Publicly Shamed*. London: Picador, p. 63ff.

8. WHAT WE WANT

1 Lockhart, J. G. (1872). *The Life of Scott*. Volume I. Edinburgh: Adam & Charles Black, p. 26.
2 Smiles, S. (1986). *Self-Help, with Illustrations of Conduct and Perseverance*. Abridged by George Bull, with an introduction by Sir Keith Joseph, Bt, MP. Harmondsworth: Penguin Books, p. 99.

3   Darwin, F. (1911). *The Life and Letters of Charles Darwin, Including an Autobiographical Chapter. Volume I*. New York: D. Appleton and Company, p. 33.
4   Smiles, A. (1956). *Samuel Smiles and his Surroundings*. London: Robert Hale, p. 26.
5   Smiles, *Self-Help*, p.16.
6   The 1986 edition was an abridged version of the 1886 edition, so the comparison that follows is between the 1986 edition and the original 1886 edition: Smiles, S. (1886). *Self-Help, with Illustrations of Conduct and Perseverance*. London: John Murray.
7   Ibid., p. 264.
8   Ibid.
9   Ibid., p. 393.
10 Ibid., p. 55.
11 Ibid., p. 41.
12 Ibid., p. 264.
13 Ibid., pp. 310–11.
14 Ibid., p. 309.
15 See, respectively, p. 166, p. 181, p. 174.
16 See, respectively, p. 244, p. 306, p. 136, p. 116, p. 288, p. 240, p. 367, p. 248.
17 Ibid., p. 99.
18 Matthew 20: 1–16.
19 Curti, M. (1967). 'The changing concept of "human nature" in the literature of American advertising', *Business History Review*, 41(4), 335–57, p. 338.
20 Strong, E. K. and Loveless, J. E. (1926). '"Want" and "solution" advertisements', *Journal of Applied Psychology*, 10(3), 346–66.
21 Hui, B., Ng, J., Berzaghi, J., Cunningham-Amos, L. and Kogan, A. (2020). 'Rewards of kindness: a meta-analysis of the link between prosociality and well-being', *Psychological Bulletin*, 146(12), 1084–116.
22 From the preface to the 1886 edition of Smiles, *Self-Help*, p. iv.

23 Rutledge, R. B., Skandali, N., Dayan, P. and Dolan, R. J. (2014). 'A computational and neural model of momentary subjective well-being', *Proceedings of the National Academy of Sciences USA*, 111, 12252–7.

9. WHERE ARE WE?

1 This was Francis Crick's 'astonishing hypothesis', which has become increasingly commonplace.
2 A few years ago, I found the same claim – 'You are your brain' – in many popular contexts (e.g. *Time, Slate Magazine, RealClearScience, Discover Magazine*), and it's easy to find similar headlines today.
3 These are just a few claims that I found in online reports of various neuroscience studies (which would have been more nuanced!): 'Your political views are "hard-wired" into your brain', *Daily Telegraph*; 'Religion is a secretion of the brain', *Bigthink.com*; 'Whether or not you believe in the paranormal may depend entirely on your brain chemistry', *New Scientist*.
4 'Scientists discover moral compass in the brain', *Daily Mail*; 'In the brain there is a center for evil', *Science News*.
5 'Racism is "hard-wired" into the brain', *Daily Mail*; 'Hard-wired to believe in God', *Daily Mail*; 'Brain scans find porn addiction', *Sunday Times*; 'Brains hard-wired to accept celebrity health advice', *Live Science*.
6 My own response to this growing mantra was a small project, 'Thinking outside the brain', which began as a talk/performance in Edinburgh in 2013. What follows is based on that, though others had made the point already. For a more detailed alternative view, see Noë, A. (2009) *Out of Our Heads: Why You are not Your Brain, and Other Lessons from the Biology of Consciousness*. New York: Hill and Wang.
7 Stephenson, K. M. (2018). 'Academic freedom, critical thinking, and

Radical Thinking

the culture of American science education.' Unpublished PhD thesis, University of Tennessee.
8   Lamont, P. (2020). 'The construction of "critical thinking": between how we think and what we believe', *History of Psychology*, 23(3), 232–51, p. 233.
9   For example: McPeck, J. E. (1981). *Critical Thinking and Education.* Oxford: Martin Robertson and Company Ltd.

10. THE LIMITS OF LOGIC

1   To keep things simple, I'm talking about deductive logic, not inductive logic. In terms of the latter, I might conclude – based on current punctuality rates – that I'll *probably* be home at 2.45. I might be confident, but I wouldn't be certain.
2   Again, to keep things simple, I'm not using formal language here. However, while we're here, let me humbly apologise to logicians for playing fast and loose with what, perhaps of all things, should be treated with greater precision. I can only hope that you can see where I'm coming from.
3   Watson, G. and Glaser, E. (1942). *Watson–Glaser Tests of Critical Thinking. Battery II: Logical Reasoning.* New York: World Book Company, p. 10.
4   It is known as 'denying the antecedent' (the 'A' being the antecedent, and the 'not' being the denying of it).
5   Lamont, P. (2020). 'The construction of critical thinking: between how we think and what we believe', *History of Psychology*, 23(3), 232–51.
6   Edwards, D. and Potter, J. (1992). *Discursive Psychology.* London: Sage, p. 50.
7   Potter, J. (1996). *Representing Reality: Discourse, Rhetoric and Social Construction.* London: Sage, p. 108.

11. THE BOUNDARIES OF SCIENCE

1   Combe, G. (1824). 'Preliminary dissertation on the progress and application of phrenology', *Transactions of the Phrenological Society*, 1, 1–65.

2   Shapin, S. (1979). 'The politics of observation: cerebral anatomy and social interests in the Edinburgh phrenology disputes', in R. Wallis, ed., *On the Margins of Science: The Social Construction of Rejected Knowledge. Sociological Review Monograph 27*. Keele: University of Keele, pp. 139–178: p.143.

3   Combe, G. (1824). 'Outlines of phrenology', *Transactions of the Phrenological Society*, 1, 75–6.

4   Spurzheim, J. C. (1825). *Phrenology, or the Doctrine of the Mind, and of the Relations between its Manifestations and the Body*. Third edition. London: Charles Knight, p. 206.

5   Roget, P. (1818). 'Cranioscopy', *Encyclopaedia Britannica*, 5th edition. Edinburgh: Constable.

6   Jeffrey, F. (1826). 'A system of phrenology', *Edinburgh Review*, 44(88), p. 253.

7   Magendie, F. (1855). *An Elementary Treatise on Human Physiology*. Translated by John Revere. New York: Harper and Brothers, p. 150.

8   [Gordon, J.] (1815). 'The doctrines of Gall and Spurzheim', *Edinburgh Review*, 25(49), p. 268.

9   Kaufman, M. H. (1999). 'Phrenology – confrontation between Spurzheim and Gordon – 1816', *Proceedings of the Royal College of Physicians*, 29, 159–70, p. 168.

10 Ibid, p. 162.

11 Shapin, 'Politics of observation', p. 160.

12 It located the mind in the brain, rather than treating it as a separate thing that was linked to the soul. It was the first approach to studying not simply the brain but differences between individual brains. It was also an attempt to understand the functions of different parts of the brain. Graham Richards calls it a 'proto-Psychology'. He also points

Radical Thinking

out that early neurologists referred to their work as a 'new phrenology': Richards, G. (2010). *Putting Psychology in its Place: Critical Historical Perspectives*. Third edition. London: Routledge, pp. 21, 121.

13 For a classic overview of the 'demarcation problem', see Laudan, L. (1996). 'The demise of the demarcation problem', in *Beyond Positivism and Relativism: Theory, Method, and Evidence*. Boulder: Westview Press, pp. 210–22.

14 Cited in Nickerson, R. (1998). 'Confirmation bias: a ubiquitous phenomenon in many guises', *Review of General Psychology*, 2(2), 175–220.

15 Cited in DuBroff, R. (2018). 'Confirmation bias, conflicts of interest and cholesterol guidance: can we trust expert opinions?', *QJM: An International Journal of Medicine*, 111(10), 687–9, p. 687.

16 Maudsley, H. (1886). *Natural Causes and Supernatural Seemings*. London: Kegan Paul, Trench & Co., p. 24.

17 Glaser, E. (1941). *An Experiment in the Development of Critical Thinking*. New York: Teachers College, Columbia University, p. 26.

18 Wason, P. C. (1960). 'On the failure to eliminate hypotheses in a conceptual task', *Quarterly Journal of Experimental Psychology*, 12(3), 129–40.

19 https://en.wikipedia.org/wiki/Peter_Cathcart_Wason.

20 This was pointed out at the time by Pierre Roget. For example, an individual might display Combativeness (a tendency to oppose or attack) yet have a small organ of Combativeness. This clearly did not fit with the claims of phrenologists. However, they could explain this by claiming that it was due to a combination of other organs. They could attribute this Combativeness to the organs of Firmness and Destructiveness. Or, perhaps, to the organ of Imitation (which led to the imitation of Combative individuals) (Leahey, T. H. and Leahey, G. E. (1984). *Psychology's Occult Doubles: Psychology and the Problem of Pseudoscience*. Chicago: Nelson-Hall, p. 83.

21 The original story can be found in Flourens, P. (1864). *Psychologie comparée*. Paris: Garnier frères, p. 234. It has been cited more recently (e.g. Bensley, A., (2002). 'Pseudoscience and science: a primer in critical thinking', in M. Shermer, ed., *The Sceptic Encyclopedia of Pseudoscience*. Santa Barbara: ABC-CLIO, p. 200) and can be found on countless websites.

22 Krech, D. (1962). 'Cortical localization of function', in L. Postman, ed., *Psychology in the Making: Histories of Selected Research Problems*. New York: Alfred. A. Knopf, p. 40.

23 In the original source, Flourens provided examples of phrenological folly, and provided sources for some of them, but provided no basis for this (Flourens, *Psychologie comparée*, p. 234).

24 Lamont, P. (2020). 'The construction of "critical thinking": between how we think and what we believe', *History of Psychology*, 23(3), 232–51, p. 236.

25 Ibid., p. 236.

26 Ibid., p. 233.

27 Wallis, W. A. (1980). 'Rejoinder', *Journal of the American Statistical Association*, 75(370), 334–5.

12. YOU CAN MAKE SENSE OF ANYTHING

1 The facts presented here are from Hunt, E. (2017). 'Trump's inauguration crowd: Sean Spicer's claims versus the evidence', *The Guardian*, 22 January. The article, of course, provided its sources.

2 These interviews are easily accessible online.

3 Newsroom (2018). 'Edinburgh named best city in the world to live', *Edinburgh Evening News*, 11 December: www.edinburghnews.scotsman.com/news/edinburgh-named-best-city-in-the-world-to-live-1425434.

4 Mcilkenny, S. (2022). 'Edinburgh named as one of the best cities to live in UK', *Edinburgh Evening News*, 19 January: www.edinburghnews.scotsman.com/news/people/edinburgh-named-as-one-of-the-best-cities-to-live-in-uk-3531875.

5 *Sunday Sport*, 24 April 1988.

6 *The Observer*, 24 April 1988.

7   *The Sun*, 21 September 1994.
8   BBC News (2016), 'Reality check: does the EU limit the number of bananas in a bunch?', 17 May, www.bbc.co.uk/news/uk-politics-eu-referendum-36316094.
9   *Sunday Sport*, 21 August 1988.
10 There are claims that are based on expert knowledge, of course, which is why we need to rely on experts. However, when such claims enter the public arena, experts do their best to explain them. And, when experts disagree, we can compare the two and spot the differences: who are these experts, what are their qualifications, and to what extent do they disagree? Even when we can't understand all the details, we can make sense of the general argument.
11 Olmsted, K. (2019). *Real Enemies: Conspiracy Theories and American Democracy, World War I to 9/11*. Oxford: Oxford University Press.
12 Bollyn, C. (2012). *Solving 9/11: The Deception that Changed the World*. USA: C. Bollyn; Griffin, D. R. (2006). *Christian Faith and The Truth Behind 9/11: A Call to Reflection and Action*. Louisville: Westminster John Knox Press; Marrs, J. (2006). *The Terror Conspiracy: Deception, 9/11, and the Loss of Liberty*. Newburyport: Red Wheel/Weiser; Ventura, J. and Russell, D. (2010). *American Conspiracies: Lies, Lies, and More Dirty Lies That the Government Tells Us*. New York: Skyhorse Publishing.

EXIT: BEYOND THE SQUARE

1   *The Post Office Annual Directory for 1825–26* (1825). Edinburgh: Printed for the Letter-carriers of the General Post Office. 1825. John Collie, Printer.